Macmillan Master Series

Accounting
Advanced English Language
Advanced Pure Mathematics
Arabic
Banking
Basic Management
Biology
British Politics
Business Administration
Business Communication
Business Law
C Programming
Catering Theory
Chemistry
COBOL Programming
Communication
Databases
Economic and Social History
Economics
Electrical Engineering
Electronic and Electrical
  Calculations
Electronics
English as a Foreign Language
English Grammar
English Language
English Literature
French
French 2
German

German 2
Global Information Systems
Human Biology
Internet
Italian
Italian 2
Japanese
Manufacturing
Marketing
Mathematics
Mathematics for Electrical and
  Electronic Engineering
Modern British History
Modern European History
Modern World History
Pascal Programming
Philosophy
Photography
Physics
Psychology
Science
Social Welfare
Sociology
Spanish
Spanish 2
Spreadsheets
Statistics
Study Skills
Visual Basic
Word Processing

Macmillan Master Series
Series Standing Order ISBN 0–333–69343–4

You can receive future titles in this series as they are published by placing a standing order. Please contact your bookseller or, in case of difficulty, write to us at the address below with your name and address, the title of the series and the ISBN quoted above.

Customer Services Department, Macmillan Distribution Ltd
Houndmills, Basingstoke, Hampshire RG21 6XS

Mastering

Visual Basic

Stephen Saxon
and
Diane Saxon

Series Editor
Timothy Davies
Computer Consultant

MACMILLAN

First published 1997 by
MACMILLAN PRESS LTD
Houndmills, Basingstoke, Hampshire RG21 6XS
and London
Companies and representatives
throughout the world

ISBN 0–333–69599–2

A catalogue record for this book is available
from the British Library.

This book is printed on paper suitable for recycling and
made from fully managed and sustained forest sources.

10   9   8   7   6   5   4   3   2   1
06   05   04   03   02   01   00   99   98   97

Copy-edited and typeset by Povey–Edmondson
Tavistock and Rochdale, England

Printed and bound in Great Britain by
Biddles Ltd
Guildford and King's Lynn

Contents

⬡ Preface

This new book in the Macmillan Mastering Series provides the essential skills needed to produce applications in the Microsoft Visual Basic language. The book builds up the necessary skills by introducing features in a logical way and providing opportunities to try them out. The features and methods are explained in easy to follow language with illustrations and graphics to help you on your way. Each chapter contains a variety of practical tasks which allow you to apply and develop your new skills.

The book is not intended to be just be another reference book – there are many perfectly good reference sources available and the on-line help available within the package is an excellent resource. The book uses a practical approach, developing the basic skills first then moving on to more advanced topics. Each chapter introduces new ideas and shows how these are used. Opportunities are provided for you to apply and practise your skills in a variety of tasks at strategic points. Practising your new skills is an important part of ensuring that you have understood the material in the chapter and helps to avoid confusion due to having too much information to process at once.

Who is this book for?

This book is for you! It is suitable for anyone who wants to learn how to write programs which run under Windows. Whether you are a home user interested in writing your own programs quickly and easily or if you are a student, this book will help you though the stages of building an application. It is suitable for students who are studying Visual Basic as part of a computing or information technology course. The book can be used by students on a variety of courses and levels who want to learn to program in Windows or are looking for extra material and perhaps a different approach to increase their understanding. Visual Basic is now present in many courses as an addition or an alternative to traditional programming. For example, it is included in GNVQ Advanced Information Technology as an additional unit and is found on many higher level courses (HNC, HND and degree level) in Business IT and Computing. Many local centres run programming courses and they are increasingly switching to Visual Basic as being the new environment for developers. City & Guilds of London provide accreditation for Visual Basic programming through their 7261 Information Technology programme.

As you reach the end of this book you will have gained a sound footing in Visual Basic programming. We hope you will have found the journey challenging and fun and will wish to continue learning and developing in Visual Basic.

STEPHEN SAXON
DIANE SAXON

Acknowledgements

The authors would like to thank our editor, Tim Davies, for his suggestions and support and Mark Saxon for checking and reading chapters. Grateful thanks are also given to Microsoft and Text 100 for providing copies of Microsoft Visual Basic software

Trademarks: Microsoft Windows, Windows 95, Visual Basic are registered trademarks of Microsoft Corporation. All brand names and product names used in this publication are trademarks, registered trademarks or tradenames of their respective holders.

Screen shots are reprinted with permission from Microsoft Corporation.

Screen shots are captured and edited using JASC Paintshop Pro.

 **Conventions**

bold	menu options
italic	new terms, first time they are introduced
typeface	commands and functions

   box   practice tasks

        points to note

1 Introduction to Visual Basic

The world of Windows programming is an exciting place to be. Microsoft Visual Basic makes it possible for anyone with a computer who is interested in joining this world to do so. This book provides the link by helping you to get started. This first chapter describes the purpose, approach and conventions used in the book. The chapter introduces the Visual Basic environment and what you will need to start producing working applications.

What do you need to get started?

You will need a copy of Microsoft Windows installed on your computer. The book shows screen shots from Windows 95 but, if you are using Windows 3.1x, your screen will not be very different from those shown in the book. You need only a basic knowledge of the Windows environment but you will find Visual Basic (and all other Windows programs) much easier to use if you have reasonable Windows and mouse skills. There are many excellent books available for Windows if you need some practice. Windows itself contains a comprehensive tutorial to help you learn what it can do and how to do it.

Not surprisingly, you will also need a copy of Visual Basic. Visual Basic is available in three versions: standard, professional and enterprise. The book assumes that you have a copy of the standard version. This is the most popular and is very affordable at around £80. The professional and enterprise editions are designed for building large corporate systems. If you have one of these editions, the information in the book is just as useful, but as well as the functions of the standard edition, you will have access to many more features. Visual Basic was announced in 1991 with the stated goal of "making developing Windows applications as easy and natural as possible. We wanted this tool to appeal to the broad mainstream of people interested in programming for Windows." Since then there have been several releases of the Visual Basic package. The latest version is version 5 which was released in 1997. Version 5 brings increased flexibility and power plus much more assistance to users and developers through the use of wizards. It contains some new controls, including controls designed for systems communicating via the Internet. Specialist books are available if you are interested in these developments.

This book is about basic skills – the controls and concepts of the language and the environment. All the skills you learn here can be used in earlier versions of Visual Basic. Later versions add new features but make only small changes to the basic features. Version 3 and 4 can run under Windows 3.1x and Windows 95. Version 4 can produce 32 bit applications running under Windows 95. Version 5 is only available to run underWindows 95, and only produces applications which run under Windows 95.

What is Visual Basic?

Visual Basic is currently the most popular language for development of Windows applications. It is widely used in the computer world in the development of a wide variety of applications. It is also used in educational and multimedia packages and can be found within the Micrsoft Office suite of applications where it forms the basis of the macro language. Visual Basic enables applications to be created with much less effort than in traditional languages. It is a complete programming language that supports the programming constructs found in most other modern programming languages.

Visual Basic is an *event driven language* because it recognizes and reacts to events. An event is an action initiated by the user. There are many possible events – for example, a mouse movement, a mouse click or a key press. Visual Basic already knows how to handle many events without needing any extra code at all. The programmer can control what happens for each event by writing code for the event.

Visual Basic is an *object oriented language* because it is based around *objects*. In their simplest form, Visual Basic objects are the building blocks which make up the screen display. Each object has its own *properties* which determine the way the object looks and behaves and its own *code* which handles the events associated with the object.

Although the code is similar to previous versions of the BASIC language, Visual Basic is quite different in approach from traditional languages. In a traditional programming language, the program leads the user through the operations in a step-by-step fashion. Programs are written in the same way – as a series of language commands which are executed one after the other. In the Visual Basic environment, the commands are attached to a particular event of an object. For example, code may be written which reacts to the user clicking a command button. As a general rule, the user is much more in command of the operation of the program and the order in which actions are executed.

Summary

In this chapter you have:

- learnt about the ideas behind Visual Basic programming
- looked at the differences between Visual Basic and traditional programming languages.

Finding your way around

This chapter aims to get you up and running as quickly as possible by giving you a quick tour of the Visual Basic environment and the windows which make up the screen display. You will also find out about the built-in help facilities and its use.

All the screen shots in this chapter are taken from Visual Basic version 5. Visual Basic versions 3 and 4 have a very different screen display where all the windows operate separately. In Visual Basic 5 the windows operate within a main Visual Basic application window. You won't find this a major problem as all versions have the basic components described here.

Getting started

When Visual Basic 5 is loaded, the screen looks something like Figure 2.1.

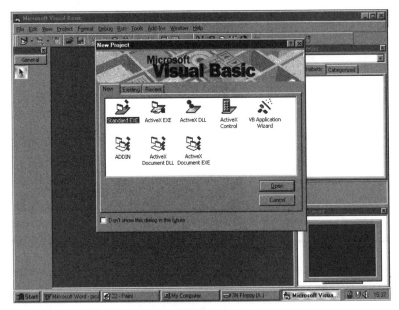

Figure 2.1

The New Project window lets you select the type of project you want to create. For most of your early applications this will be a standard Visual Basic project.

Select the Standard EXE option and let's have a look at the environment.

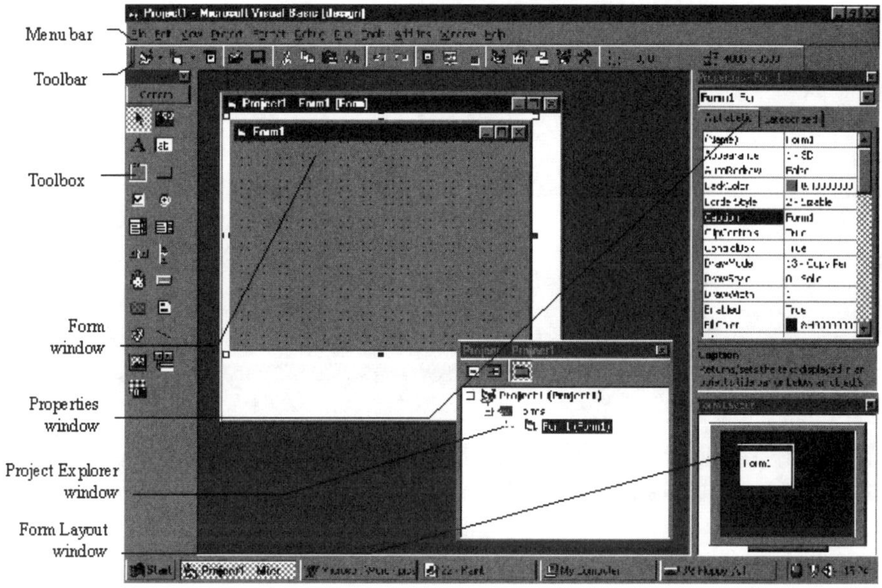

Figure 2.2

The screen display shown in Figure 2.2 shows the basic screen components. The windows you will need when creating projects are the Form window, the Toolbox, the Properties window and the Project Explorer window.

Customizing the display

Like most Windows applications, Visual Basic can be customized so much that it can be made to look very different from that shown in the figure. Again, this won't be a problem as the basic components will be there somewhere!

All windows and toolbars in Visual Basic can be moved to different parts of the screen, and docked against the sides. In Figure 2.2, the Properties window is docked to the right-hand side, the Toolbox to the left-hand, the toolbar to the top of the window and the Form window is left floating in the middle. They can be moved by clicking inside the window and dragging to a different part of the screen. Another possible arrangement is shown in Figure 2.3 where all the items are floating.

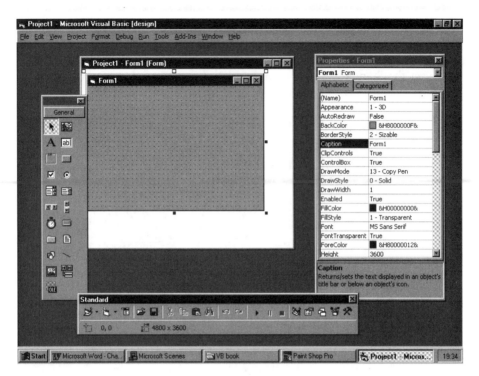

Figure 2.3

If you do not want a window to dock against the side, it is possible to force it to be floating. Click with the right mouse button on the window and deselect the dockable option.

The various windows can be moved to any part of the screen and you can change their sizes to suit your own preferences and needs.

Displaying windows

Each part of the display has its own Close box so you can remove it from the screen by clicking on the ▣ in the top right of the window.

To open it again, you can use the buttons on the toolbar, as shown in Figure 2.4.

Another way of doing this is to use the **View** menu shown in Figure 2.5.

The screen display normally shows the Standard toolbar. The **Toolbars** option from this menu determines the toolbars which are visible. For most work, the standard toolbar is fine, but other toolbars (for example the Debug toolbar) are useful at different times.

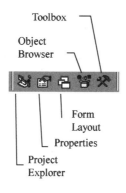

Toolbox

Object
Browser

Form
Layout

Properties

Project
Explorer

Figure 2.4

⊞	<u>C</u>ode	
⊟	O<u>b</u>ject	Shift+F7
	<u>D</u>efinition	Shift+F2
	Last Position	Ctrl+Shift+F2
🎥	<u>O</u>bject Browser	F2
🔲	<u>I</u>mmediate Window	Ctrl+G
⊞	Local<u>s</u> Window	
🔍	Watc<u>h</u> Window	
🔧	Call St<u>a</u>ck...	Ctrl+L
🔧	<u>P</u>roject Explorer	Ctrl+R
📋	Properties <u>W</u>indow	F4
🔧	<u>F</u>orm Layout Window	
	Property Pa<u>g</u>es	Shift+F4
🔧	Toolbo<u>x</u>	
	Color Pa<u>l</u>ette	
	<u>T</u>oolbars	▶

Figure 2.5

As you can see, the arrangement of the Visual Basic environment is completely up to you. All the screen shots in the book use a standard setup, but your screen will look different depending on how you have configured Visual Basic.

Task 2.1   Exploring the environment

Load Visual Basic and choose Standard EXE. Try moving all the different windows and toolbars. Try docking windows and toolbars to different edges of the screen.

Use the **View** menu to investigate the windows contained in Visual Basic. You will use them later, so it is a good idea to familiarize yourself with the layout now.

Parts of the screen display

Form window

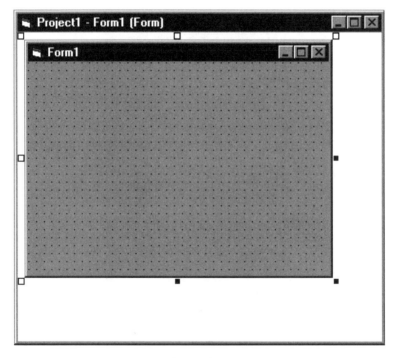

Figure 2.6

The form, as in Figure 2.6, is the basic element in Visual Basic. An application can have one or many forms. The form is a display area where the application program works. It is a window in which you place controls to create your screen display. The appearance of the form is controlled by setting its properties. The form can have code attached to it which will run when the form is loaded or closed or moved.

Toolbox

The Toolbox is shown in Figure 2.7. It contains the set of *controls* which make up a Visual Basic application. These controls allow you to display information on the screen, use Windows features such as *drop down boxes* and *check boxes* and add interest to your screens through graphics.

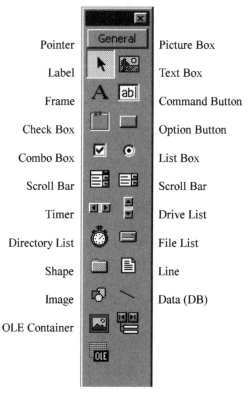

Figure 2.7

The Toolbox appears confusing at first but you will soon get to know what each tool does and how to use it. Visual Basic provides help with identifying the controls through Tooltips. This list of tools may help you to get started.

Tool	Description
Pointer	selects objects
Label	displays text
Frame	groups controls together
Check box	acts as a switch
Combo box	displays list of values
Scroll bar	sets values
Timer	controls timed actions
Shape	draws shapes
Image	displays pictures
Picture box	displays pictures and groups graphics
Text box	displays text and accepts input
Command button	selects an action
Option button	selects an option from a group
List box	displays a list of items
Line	draws lines

```
Properties - Form1                    ⊠
Form1  Form                           ▼
 Alphabetic │ Categorized │
(Name)          │ Form1              │▲
Appearance      │ 1 - 3D            │
AutoRedraw      │ False             │
BackColor       │ ▣ &H8000000F&     │
BorderStyle     │ 2 - Sizable       │
Caption         │ Form1             │
ClipControls    │ True              │
ControlBox      │ True              │
DrawMode        │ 13 - Copy Pen     │
DrawStyle       │ 0 - Solid         │
DrawWidth       │ 1                 │
Enabled         │ True              │
FillColor       │ ■ &H00000000&     │
FillStyle       │ 1 - Transparent   │
Font            │ MS Sans Serif     │
FontTransparent │ True              │
ForeColor       │ ■ &H80000012&     │
Height          │ 3600              │
HelpContextID   │ 0                 │
Icon            │ (Icon)            │
KeyPreview      │ False             │
Left            │ 0                 │
LinkMode        │ 0 - None          │▼
Caption
Returns/sets the text displayed in an object's
title bar or below an object's icon.
```

Figure 2.8

Every control has properties which affect its appearance. The Properties window as in Figure 2.8 shows all the properties of the selected control. The window can be sized to increase the number of properties which can be seen at once. Some controls have too many properties for this to be possible and you will then have scroll bars at the right-hand side of the window so that all the properties can be viewed. A brief description of the currently selected property is at the bottom of the window. You will find out much more about controls in the next chapter.

Project Explorer window

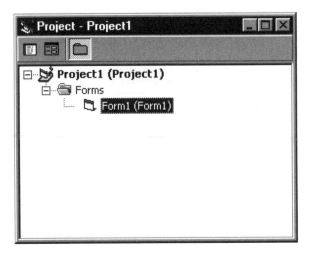

Figure 2.9

The project holds all the forms, controls and code procedures which make up the application. The parts of the project can be seen in the Project Explorer window as in Figure 2.9. Projects are covered in more detail in Chapter 4.

Form Layout window

The Form Layout window, shown in Figure 2.10, shows the position of the form on the screen. To move the form, click on it in the Form Layout window and drag it to a new position.

Figure 2.10

The Form Layout window is useful if you have more than one form and want to position them so that both are visible. The use of multiple forms is covered in Chapter 16.

Visual Basic Help

Visual Basic has an excellent built-in Help system. The help menu is shown in Figure 2.11.

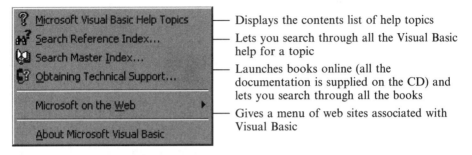

Microsoft Visual Basic Help Topics	— Displays the contents list of help topics
Search Reference Index...	— Lets you search through all the Visual Basic help for a topic
Search Master Index...	
Obtaining Technical Support...	— Launches books online (all the documentation is supplied on the CD) and lets you search through all the books
Microsoft on the Web ▶	— Gives a menu of web sites associated with Visual Basic
About Microsoft Visual Basic	

Figure 2.11

Tutorial

Earlier versions of Visual Basic contain a tutorial which helps new users to get to know the package. This is accessed from the **Help** menu. Figure 2.12 shows the starting screen of the tutorial from Version 4.

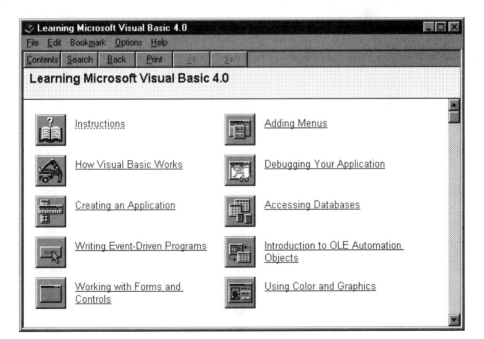

Figure 2.12

The tutorial has a series of lessons which take you through many of the features of the package. Each lesson has a number of screens which can be printed out for reference.

The level of information presented in the tutorial is quite detailed and you are advised to defer working through this in any depth until you have more knowledge of the basics of Visual Basic.

The tutorial is not available in this pre-release version of Visual Basic 5 but is likely to be present when Visual Basic 5 is released.

Help topics

The Visual Basic Help Topics option shown in Figure 2.13 provides access to the help by topic. Each topic can be opened to display sub-topics which can be opened in turn until the help screens are reached.

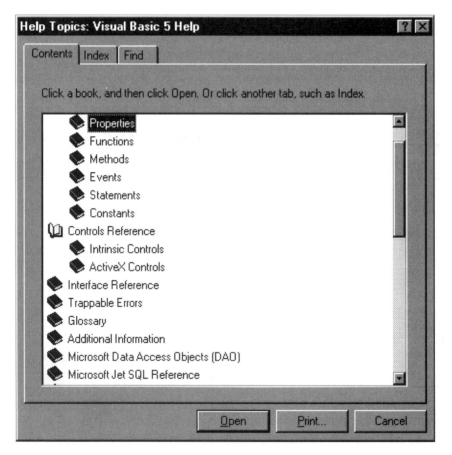

Figure 2.13

Reference index

The Search Reference Index option gives a list of all the help topics that are available. This is a very long list! To get help on a particular topic, type a related word into the box at the top and select a relevant topic from the list.

To display a topic you select the topic from the list and click on Display.

Task 2.2   Using Help

Enter "Properties" in the index search and try to find help about the Properties window, as shown in Figure 2.14.

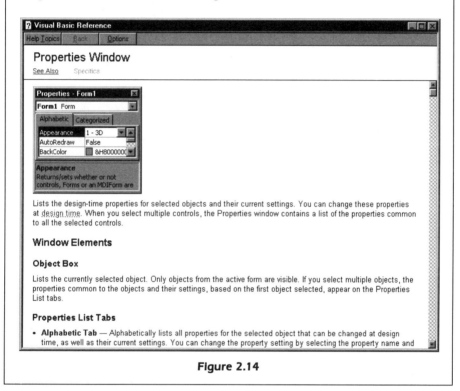

Figure 2.14

Master index

In version 5 the Search Master Index option provides access to the online books feature. This allows fast access to all the documentation in the Visual Basic package. Information can be accessed by topic or by searching. More details of the online books facilities can be found in Appendix A at the end of this book.

Context-sensitive help

Context-sensitive help means that the help screens are directly relevant to the item you are currently working on. Context-sensitive help is accessed by pressing F1. It then automatically locates and displays the relevant topic.

── **Task 2.3 Context-sensitive Help** ──────────────

Select the form window and press F1. This will display help connected with the Form window, as shown in Figure 2.15.

```
┌─────────────────────────────────────────────────────────────┐
│ ? Visual Basic Reference                           _ □ X     │
├─────────────────────────────────────────────────────────────┤
│ Help Topics │  Back   │  Options                             │
├─────────────────────────────────────────────────────────────┤
│ Form Object, Forms Collection                                │
│ See Also    Example    Properties   Methods   Events  Specifics │
│ ───────────────────────────────────────────────────────────  │
│ A Form object is a window or dialog box that makes up part of an application's user interface. │
│                                                               │
│ A Forms collection is a collection whose elements represent each loaded form in an application. The collection │
│ includes the application's MDI form, MDI child forms, and non-MDI forms. The Forms collection has a single │
│ property, Count, that specifies the number of elements in the collection. │
│                                                               │
│ Syntax                                                        │
│ Form                                                          │
│ Forms(index)                                                  │
│ The placeholder index represents an integer with a range from 0 to Forms.Count - 1. │
│                                                               │
│ Remarks                                                       │
│ You can use the Forms collection to iterate through all loaded forms in an application. It identifies an intrinsic │
│ global variable named Forms. You can pass Forms(index) to a function. whose argument is specified as a │
│ Forms class.                                                  │
│                                                               │
│ Forms have properties that determine aspects of their appearance, such as position, size, and color; and │
│ aspects of their behavior, such as whether or not they are resizable. │
│                                                               │
│ Forms can also respond to events initiated by a user or triggered by the system. For example, you could write │
│ code in a form's Click event procedure that would enable the user to change the color of a form by clicking it. │
│                                                               │
│ In addition to properties and events, you can use methods to manipulate forms using code. For example, you │
│ can use the Move method to change a form's location and size. │
│                                                               │
│ A special kind of form, the MDI form, can contain other forms called MDI child forms. An MDI form is created │
│ with the MDI Form command on the Insert menu; an MDI child form is created by choosing New Form from the │
│ File menu and then setting the MDIChild property to True. │
└─────────────────────────────────────────────────────────────┘
```

Figure 2.15

The Help system is also very useful for providing assistance when you are writing program code. It gives the detailed format of each command (called the syntax) and helps you to get the command correct. Using help in this way will be covered later in the book.

Summary

In this chapter you have:

- been introduced to the Visual Basic environment and its building blocks
- learnt about the different parts of the display
- seen how to customize the screen display
- used Visual Basic built-in help.

Using Forms

This chapter looks at the form – the basic building block of Visual Basic. The form can be thought of as a window which looks and behaves much like other windows you will have used in other applications.

What is a form?

The *form* is the central part of Visual Basic. It provides the display area for the application. The form acts as the container for all the controls which make up the application. Both a form and the controls on a form have code attached to them.

The default form in Visual Basic is named Form1. When the program is first loaded you will see a blank form as in Figure 3.1.

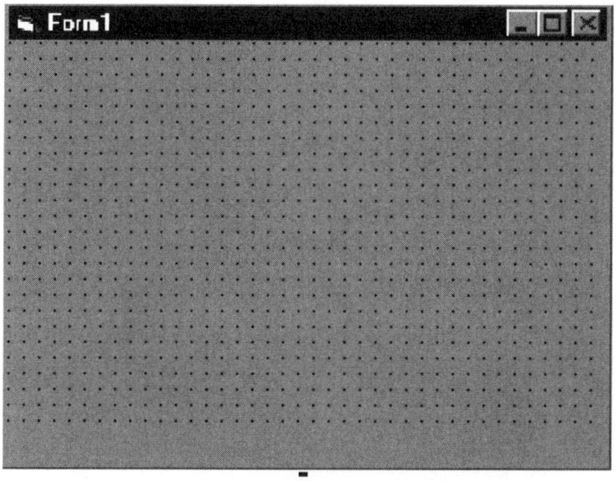

Figure 3.1

Depending on the version you are using and the way it is set up, there may be other windows on your screen. However, you should be able to see the form as shown somewhere on the screen. The dots on the form are the *grid*. These help you to draw and place controls on the form by forcing the edges of controls to line up with the dots of the grid.

Introduction to properties

In the last chapter you discovered the properties window and learned that all Visual Basic components have a set of properties which govern the way they look and behave. The Form is no exception to this and has its own set of properties which determine the appearance and behaviour of the form. The Form properties are shown in Figure 3.2.

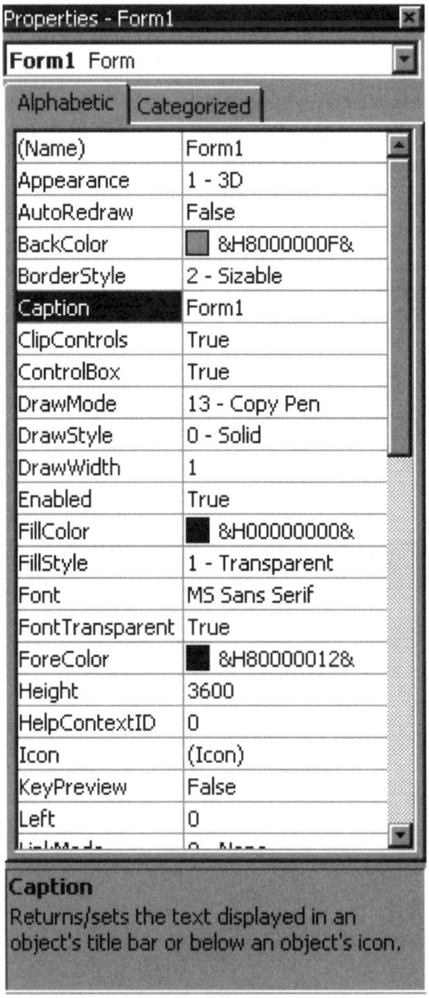

Figure 3.2

This is quite an impressive list. Scroll up and down the list and have a look at the properties available. An important point to notice at this stage is that each property has a value. These are the *default* settings for the property and will apply unless you change them. This means that Visual Basic knows about the form without you having to do anything at all – a far cry from traditional programming languages where the programmer does all the work.

Earlier versions presented the properties in an alphabetical list. Version 5 allows you to view the list in different ways. The tabs at the top of the properties window let you choose which of the two views you want. The view shown in Figure 3.2 is an alphabetical list, but often it is easier if the properties are grouped by type. Click on the Categorized tab at the top of the Properties window. It will then look like Figure 3.3.

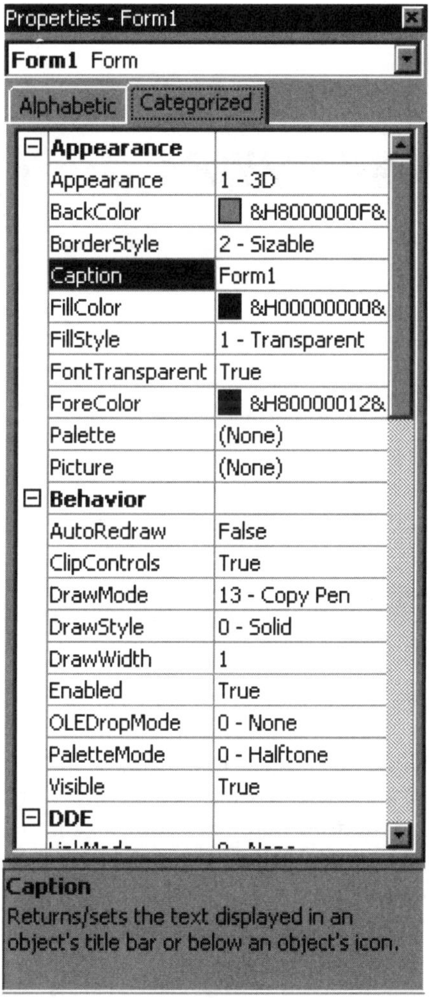

Properties - Form1	☒
Form1 Form	▼

Alphabetic	Categorized

⊟ **Appearance**		▲
Appearance	1 - 3D	
BackColor	▨ &H8000000F&	
BorderStyle	2 - Sizable	
Caption	Form1	
FillColor	▩ &H00000000&	
FillStyle	1 - Transparent	
FontTransparent	True	
ForeColor	▩ &H80000012&	
Palette	(None)	
Picture	(None)	
⊟ **Behavior**		
AutoRedraw	False	
ClipControls	True	
DrawMode	13 - Copy Pen	
DrawStyle	0 - Solid	
DrawWidth	1	
Enabled	True	
OLEDropMode	0 - None	
PaletteMode	0 - Halftone	
Visible	True	
⊟ **DDE**		
LinkMode	0 - None	▼

Caption
Returns/sets the text displayed in an object's title bar or below an object's icon.

Figure 3.3

The categories of properties are shown in bold. By clicking on the + and – signs by the categories, they can be expanded or reduced so it is easier to work with particular groups of properties.

Running the program

── Task 3.1 Running ──────────────────────────────────

To prove that this form works without doing anything else, you can *run* the program.

Click on the Run icon on the toolbar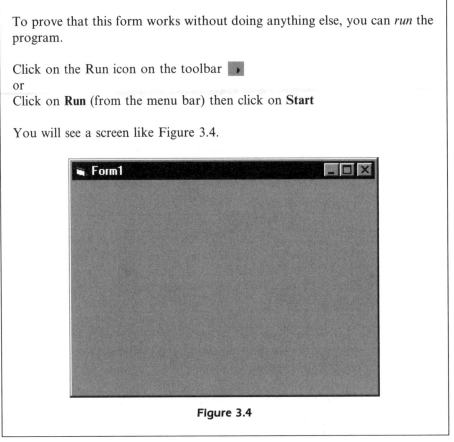
or
Click on **Run** (from the menu bar) then click on **Start**

You will see a screen like Figure 3.4.

Figure 3.4

There is not a lot of change from the original appearance of the form but you will notice that the dots are no longer visible. Remember that these are the grid and are only needed to help you draw and place controls on the form. The form has a Title bar saying Form1, a control menu box at the left of the Title bar and a set of Minimize, Maximize and Close buttons at the right of the Title bar.

Try out the Maximize and Minimize buttons and see what happens.

You will have found that these do exactly what you would expect them to do – they are standard Windows features. The clever part is that they are here in your Visual Basic application without you programming them in.

Now move your mouse to the Title bar and try moving the Form window to a different position on the screen. Then try moving your mouse to the corners and sides of the Form window and try sizing the Form window.

As before, the form window behaves exactly as you would expect – and you still haven't done any programming.

This is the basis of the power of Visual Basic – many operations and functions can be achieved with very little effort from the programmer. You will see more and more of this power as your knowledge develops in the coming chapters.

Stopping the program

Click on the End icon on the toolbar ▪
or
Click on **Run** then click on **End**

This returns the form to its original appearance – check that the dots are back. When the form looks like this you are in *design mode*. The Visual Basic Title bar will say [Design].

Designing your form

You have seen the default Visual Basic form – the version without any changes. Look at the Properties window in Figure 3.2 again. Of this large number of properties, some are used nearly every time you create a form while some are used much less often.

The most important properties for a form are:

Property	Settings
Appearance	determines the type of window 0 – Flat (like Windows 3.1) 1 – 3D (like Windows 95)
BackColor	sets the background color of the form. This is grey for 3D forms and white for Flat forms or for earlier versions of Visual Basic. Pastel colors are best
BorderStyle	determines whether the form has a border or can be sized
Caption	sets the text of the Title bar
ControlBox	determines whether a control menu box appears at the left of the Title bar
Height	sets the height of the form
Left	sets the position of the left-hand edge of the form

Property	Settings
MaxButton	determines whether the form has a Maximize button
MinButton	determines whether the form has a Minimize button
(Name)	used by Visual Basic to identify the form
Top	sets the position of the Top of the form
Width	sets the width of the form

Setting form properties

The properties can be changed in two ways:

Select the property by clicking on it. For some properties, this displays an arrow to the right of the property. If you click on this arrow you get a list of all the different values the property can take. Select the required option from the list.

The other way is to double-click on the property. This cycles through all the different styles and types. Double-clicking is usually quicker than selecting from the list. Many properties are either On or Off. This is indicated by True or False in Visual Basic.

Other properties require you to type a value. The value will appear on the line in the Properties window.

Most of the properties are self-explanatory. You can find out what a property does by trying it out – setting the property and then running the program to see what it does. You can also use the on-line help. To get help on a property, select the property in the list and press F1. Don't be afraid to experiment with different properties – you can't break it!

___ **Task 3.2   Experimenting with properties** _____

- Try out the following property settings for the form.
- Make the changes to the property settings one by one.
- Run the form to see what happens.
- Stop the program (from the toolbar or menu) and make the next change.

Appearance – Flat
BackColor – any pale color of your choice
Caption – your name and the date
ControlBox – False (versions 3 and 4 MaxButton and MinButton False)
Height – 5000

Figure 3.5 shows an example of how your form may look.

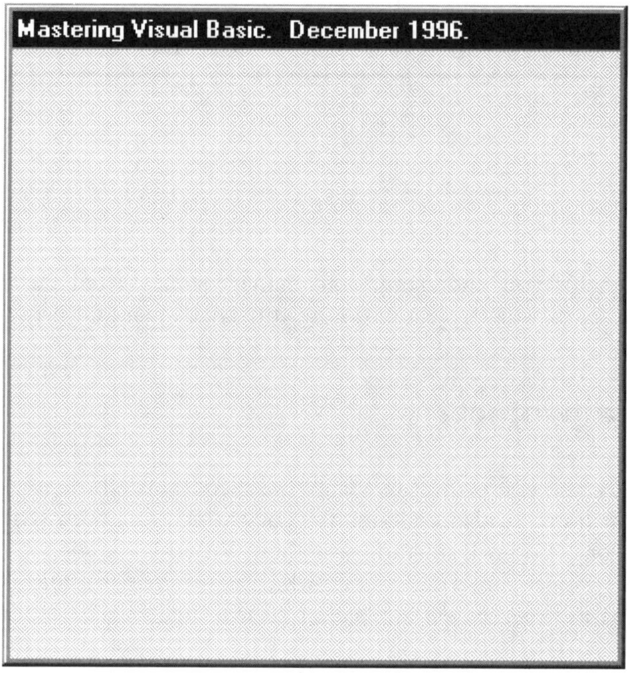

Mastering Visual Basic. December 1996.

Figure 3.5

Summary

This chapter has introduced the following topics:

- the Visual Basic form
- running a program
- stopping a program
- properties of the form
- changing properties.

Working with projects

This chapter helps you understand and manage your Visual Basic projects. It deals with the parts of a project and how you save, open and print projects.

What is a project?

As you already know, a project in Visual Basic contains all the forms that make up your application. It also contains the code which has been written to make those forms work. You will start to learn about Visual Basic code in the following chapters. The project can contain code which is on the form and code which is written in separate *code modules*. Chapter 17 investigates code modules.

The Project Explorer window

The Project Explorer window is one of the basic screen elements. It shows all the parts of the project. When you start a new project the project window is as shown in Figure 4.1. It contains only an entry for Form1. Form1 is the name Visual Basic gives to the first form in any new project.

Figure 4.1

As you work on the project, the project window will have more entries. The sample in Figure 4.2 shows a project with several forms and a code module. Forms and modules have different icons. This is useful, particularly in earlier versions of Visual Basic, as it helps to identify the parts of the project. As you would expect, the project window can be sized to display more or fewer entries. If there are more entries than can fit in the window, scroll bars will appear. As for the properties window, the + and − signs can be used to give a summary view of the contents of the project.

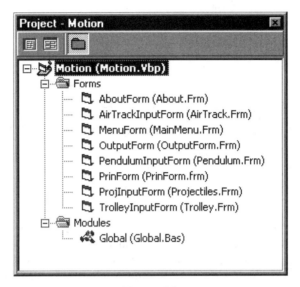

Figure 4.2

You can use the project window to open forms so you can work on them. Highlight the required file in the project window. Click on View Code ▣ or View Form ▣ buttons.

Saving a project

You will be creating many projects as you work through this book. As Visual Basic can only have one project open at a time, you must save each project with a different name if you wish to use them again. Some of the projects are small demonstrations and you will probably not want to bother saving them. However some of the longer projects involve quite a lot of work in setting up the form and controls and writing code so you are advised to save them as you work through the activities.

Click on **File**
Click on **Save Project**
or
Click on the Save icon on the toolbar ▣

This displays the Save Project As dialog box, as in Figure 4.3.

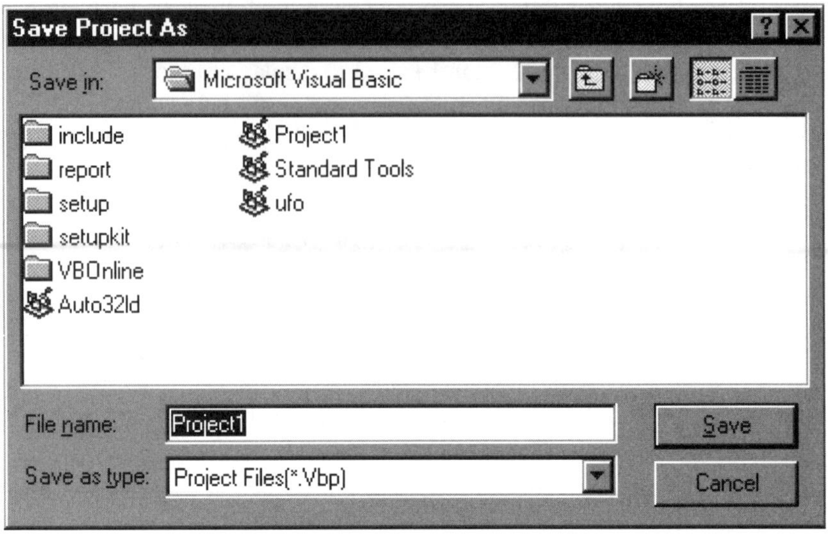

Figure 4.3

By default, Visual Basic saves the project in the Visual Basic folder with a name of Project1. You may wish to save your projects in your Windows 95 My Documents folder as this keeps it with all your other work, and makes it easier to back up your work. You will certainly want to change the name of the project. Use a name which reflects the nature of the project. Windows 95 makes this much easier!

Visual Basic will also prompt you to save each individual component of the project. These are saved as separate files. Visual Basic knows whether the file is a form or a code module and automatically adds the correct extension. These are:

FRM	Form
BAS	Code module
VBP	Project
VBG	Project Group

Earlier versions of Visual Basic used MAK as the file extension for the project.

Opening a project

Click on **File**

Click on **Open Project**

or

Click on the Open icon on the toolbar 📂

This displays the Open Project dialog box shown in Figure 4.4.

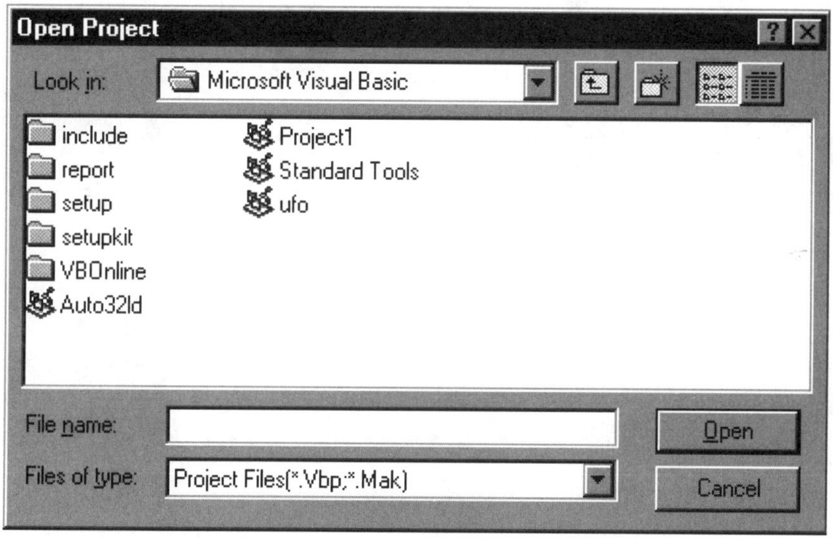

Figure 4.4

If you already have a project open, Visual Basic will check to see if you want to save it before starting the new project.

Opening the .VBP or .MAK file opens all the elements of the project.

Opening more than one project

Visual Basic allows you to have more than one project open at a time. Click on the Add Project icon 📑 ▾ on the toolbar to add a new standard EXE project with a blank Form1. Click on **File** then **Add Project** to add an existing project. The Project Explorer window will now show the component parts of all the open projects. These can be saved as a group if required.

Starting a new project

Click on **File**
Click on **New Project**

This will display a New Project dialog, as shown in Figure 4.5.

Figure 4.5

This is a list of all the different application types which you can create in Visual Basic. Standard EXE is the option which allows you to create normal Windows applications.

> Do not worry if your New Project window does not have as many options in it. It depends upon which version of Visual Basic you are running and the options installed.

Another way of starting a new project is to click on the New icon on the toolbar ⬚. The arrow to the right of the icon lets you select the project type.

Either of these ways creates a new project with a blank Form1 ready for you to start work. As before, any existing open projects will be closed and you will be prompted to save any changes.

Running a project

You already know how to run a project to see the effects of the property settings. There are three ways of doing this:

- using the toolbar icons ▶ ‖ ■
  Run Pause Stop
- using menu options
- using key shortcuts

Start

Click on the Run icon on the toolbar ▶
or
Click on **Run** then click on **Start**
or
Press F5

The toolbar icons change when the program is running ▶ ‖ ■.

   You can now select Stop to stop the program running and return to design mode or you can click Pause.

Stop

Click on the Stop icon on the toolbar
or
Click on **Run** then click on **Stop**
or
Hold down Shift and press F5

Pause

▶ ‖ ■

When the project is paused, it is in *Break mode*. In Break mode you can use the debugging facilities of Visual Basic. These are covered in Chapter 12.

To continue execution:
Click on the Run icon
or
Click on **Run** then click on **Continue**

To stop execution:
Click on the End icon on the toolbar ■
or
Click on **Run** then on **End**.

Printing a project

Click on **File** then on **Print**.

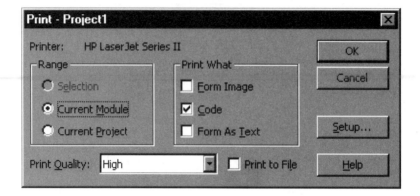

Figure 4.6

From the dialog box, as in Figure 4.6, select the parts of the project to be printed.

The Print What section allows you to select:

Form Image	produces a graphical image of the form
Form As Text	prints the properties of the form and its controls
Code	prints all the event code you have written

The Range section allows you to specify which parts of the project are to be printed:

Selection	prints the currently selected code.
Current Module	prints the forms and/or code for the currently selected module.
Project	prints the forms and/or code for the entire project

Summary

This chapter has covered:

- the Visual Basic project and its components
- saving projects
- opening projects
- starting new projects
- running projects
- printing projects.

⬡ 5   **Exploring controls**

So far, you have only seen forms. A form is not very useful on its own. With controls, you can add text boxes, labels and buttons to your form and begin to make the forms do something!

What is a control?

A control is an object which is placed on to a form. Without controls, a form cannot do anything. Controls make it possible for the form to interact with the user. This may be clicking on a button or entering text into a text box. Once controls have been placed on a form, code can be added to them (you'll find out how in the next chapter), and this enables you to build working applications.

A control has a set of properties, similar to a form. Each type of control has different properties associated with it. Using the properties of a control, its function and appearance can be changed.

One of the properties of all controls is its name. Every control needs to have a unique name. Visual Basic will allocate a name to each control as it is created. You have already seen that the form is called Form1. Controls are named with the type of the control followed by a sequential number. You will find out much more about controls and their names as you work through this chapter.

Placing controls on a form

Controls are selected from the Toolbox. The standard edition of Visual Basic provides a good range of controls and includes all the basic Windows features. If you have the professional edition, there will be many more available.

Figure 5.1 shows the controls in the standard version of Visual Basic.

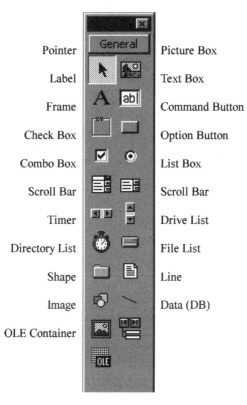

Figure 5.1

Only some of these will be covered in this chapter: label, text box and command button.

To draw a control on a form:

- Select the control from the toolbox
- Move the mouse over the form area. The cursor will change to a cross.
- Click and hold down the left mouse button at the top left of where you would like the control.
- Drag the mouse to the bottom right and release the button.

Another way to place a control on a form is to double-click the tool in the Toolbox. This will place a default sized control in the centre of the form.

Moving and sizing controls

Once you have drawn a control on the form, you will probably want to adjust its size and position. This is done in a similar way to most drawing programs.

- Firstly, the control must be selected. Use the pointer tool from the toolbox  to select the control on the form.
- When a control is selected, blue dots called *handles* will appear around the control, as in Figure 5.2.

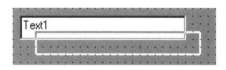

Figure 5.2

- The control can be moved by clicking anywhere inside the control and dragging it to a new position before releasing the mouse button, as in Figure 5.3.

Figure 5.3

- The control can be sized by clicking on the blue handles at the sides and corners of the shape (the mouse pointer will change to a sizing arrow) and dragging, as in Figure 5.4.

Figure 5.4

Controls placed by double clicking can be moved and sized in the same way.

Task 5.1 Drawing controls

Start a new project with a blank form. Try selecting different controls from the toolbox and placing them on to the form. An example is shown in Figure 5.5.

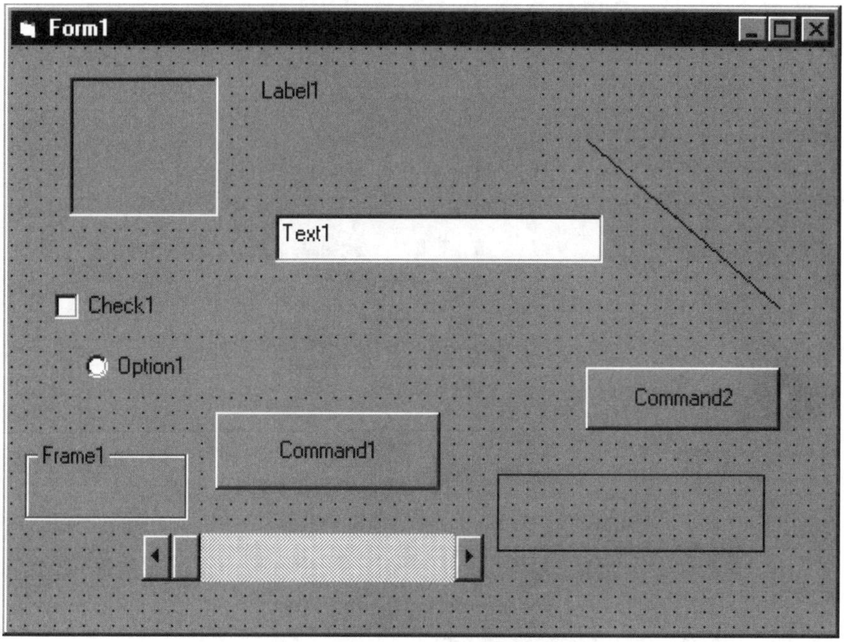

Figure 5.5

Practise moving and sizing the controls you have drawn.

Selecting many controls

It is possible to select more than one control at a time. This is useful if you want to move the controls together or change the same property of many controls at once.

You can use the pointer tool to select many controls by clicking at one corner of the group and dragging the pointer around all the controls, as shown in Figure 5.6.

If the objects you want to select are not all in a group, you can select multiple objects by holding down the Ctrl key and clicking on the objects you want to select, as in Figure 5.7.

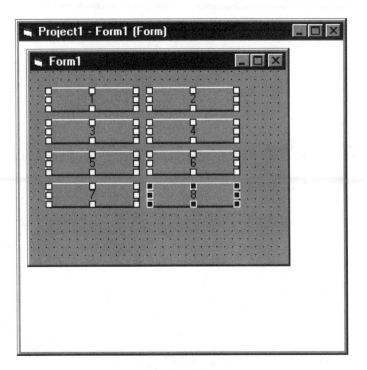

Figure 5.6

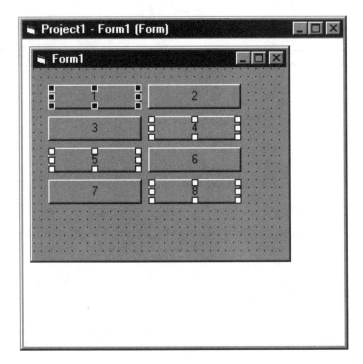

Figure 5.7

Aligning controls

It is often difficult to line up your controls and make them the same size on the form. Visual Basic has a number of options on the **Format** menu to help you.

Select two (or more) controls using the above techniques, and then you can force the objects to be the same size, or take the same positions on the form. All the different options are available as sub-menus of the **Format** menu.

Copying controls

If you want many controls which are the same size and have the same properties on a form, you can Cut, Copy and Paste them using the Windows clipboard.

To copy a control:

- Select the control on the form by clicking on it
- Choose **Copy** from the **Edit** menu
- Click on the form to deselect the control
- Choose **Paste** from the **Edit** menu

You will see a dialog box, as in Figure 5.8.

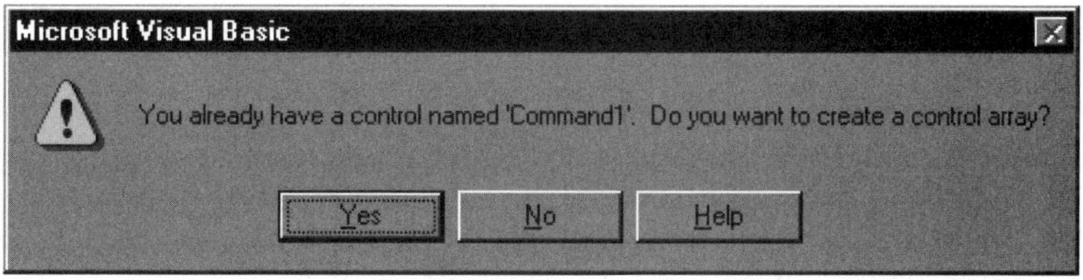

Microsoft Visual Basic

You already have a control named 'Command1'. Do you want to create a control array?

Yes   No   Help

Figure 5.8

This is not as cryptic as it seems. A control array is a set of similar controls which all have the same name. This will be covered in Chapter 15.

- Click No to create a new control.

The pasted control has the same shape, size and properties as the original. Visual Basic gives a new name to the pasted control. You will then need to move this to the required position.

Labels

A

The label control is used for displaying information on the form. The user cannot enter anything into a label. It is for *output* of information only.

The label control is the letter A in the toolbox. It is placed on to a form in the standard way outlined above.

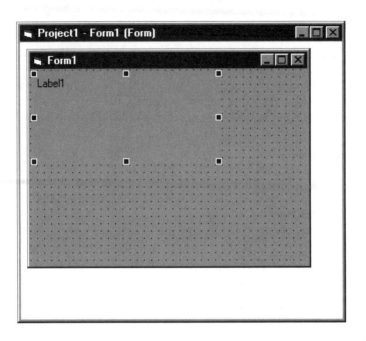

Figure 5.9

Initially, it is just a box with Label1 written inside it, as shown in Figure 5.9. The label control has properties which affect the way it looks and behaves. These properties are accessed from the properties window. You can click on the properties window if it is visible, click on the ![button] button on the toolbar, or press F4 when the label is selected. Any of these ways will show the properties for the label, as in Figure 5.10.

This is a very daunting list of properties! Thankfully, most of them are seldom used so this chapter concentrates on the most useful properties. Many properties are self-explanatory. You can find out about them by trying out the different properties, and using the on-line help. To get help on a property, select the property from the list and press F1.

Naming the label

The Name property (in brackets in Visual Basic 5) is the name Visual Basic uses to identify this particular label. As you now know, every form and control must have a unique name. The Name property cannot contain any spaces. By default Visual Basic will allocate names to your controls using Label1, followed by Label2, Label3 and so on. These are not very descriptive names so it is much better to give your controls a more meaningful name. For example, if it was a welcome message in a label, you might set the name property to 'lblWelcome'. More explanation about naming conventions is contained later in this chapter.

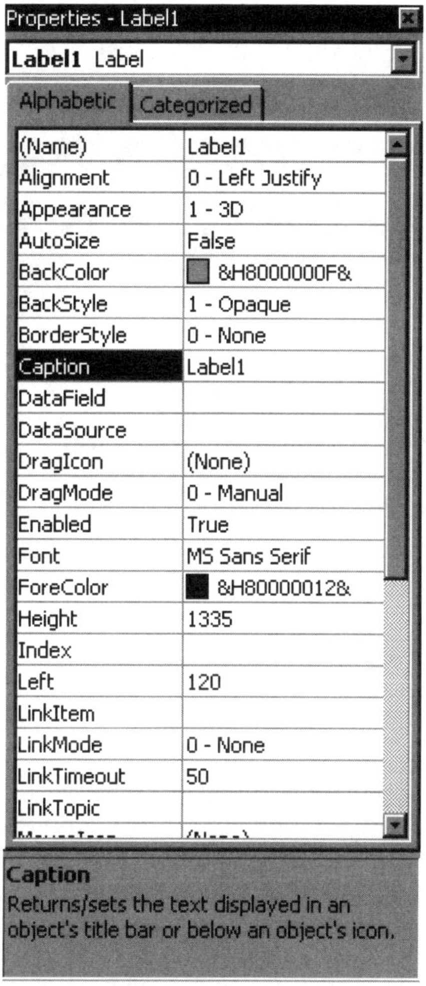

Figure 5.10

To change the name of a label, click on the (Name) property and type the new name.

The (Name) property did not have brackets around it in Visual Basic versions 3 and 4.

Entering text

The caption property specifies the text to be displayed inside the label. By default, this will be the name, for example Label1, but you will always want to change it to your particular message. To change the text, select the caption property from the

Properties window and start typing. As you type in the Properties window, the changes are automatically displayed in the label at the same time, as in Figure 5.11.

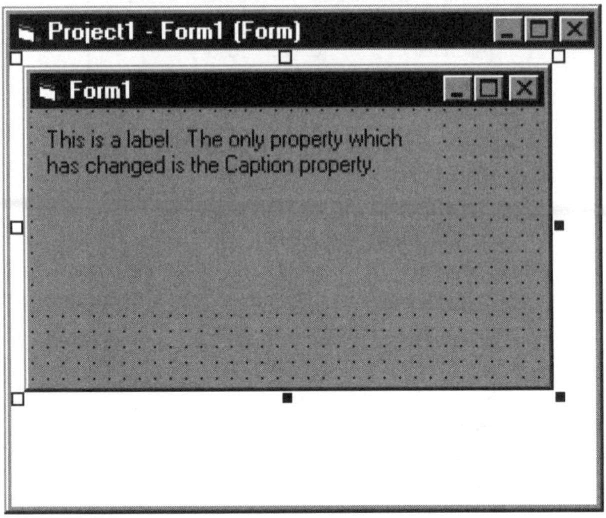

Figure 5.11

Adding a border

Borders are controlled by two properties: BorderStyle and Appearance. The BorderStyle property sets whether or not the label has a border, and the appearance property sets the type of border.

The property can be changed in two ways:

Select the property by clicking on it. This will display an arrow at the right of the property. If you click on this arrow you get a list of all the different values the property can take. Select the required option from the list, as shown in Figure 5.12.

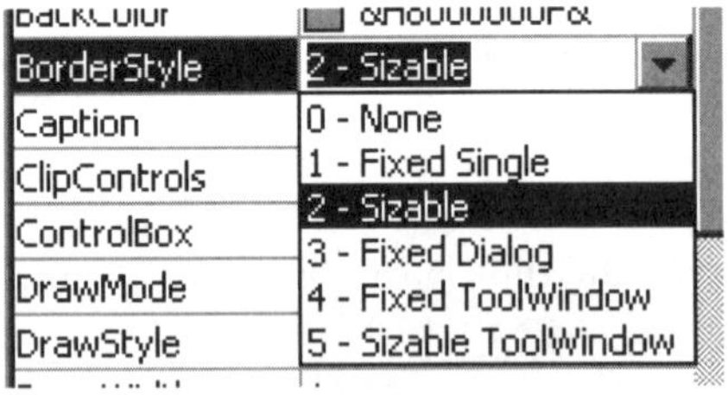

Figure 5.12

The other way is to double-click on the property. This cycles through all the different styles and types. Double-clicking is usually quicker than selecting from the list.

Examples of labels with different borders are shown in Figure 5.13.

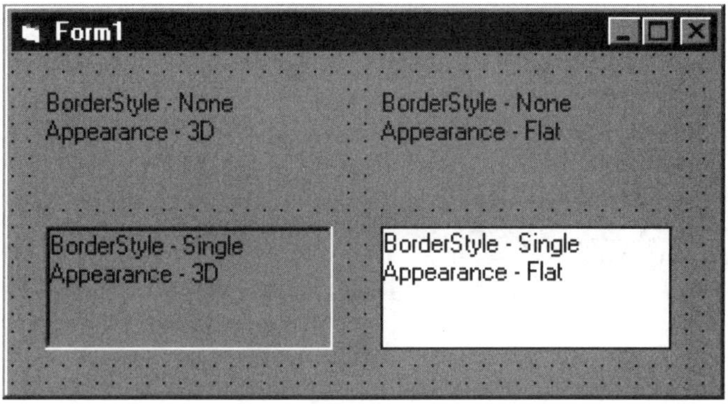

Figure 5.13

The background color of the label changes when you select Flat. This is because Windows 3.1 applications used flat, white windows, and these have white backgrounds. Windows 95 windows are usually 3D and grey, so the 3D option defaults to a grey background.

Colors

The background color is set by the BackColor property. You will notice that this has a strange code in it, as in Figure 5.14.

BackColor   &H8000000F&

Figure 5.14

This is a special way Visual Basic uses to refer to a color. It is a hexadecimal number which specifies how much red, green and blue is contained in the color. Don't worry though, you do not need to learn these codes. You can change the color from a color selection box which is activated either by clicking on the property name and then on the arrow at the right, or more easily by double-clicking on the property name. The color selection box is shown in Figure 5.15.

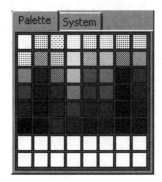

Figure 5.15

There are two sets of colors. The System option lets you access the colors which are set up through Control Panel, and so the user can change them. It is more usual to use the Palette colors.

Visual Basic 3 and 4 users will not have the System option, and can only select from the palette of colors.

The foreground color (the color of the text) is specified by the ForeColor property. You can change this in the same way as for the BackColor above.

Font

Visual Basic allows you to use any of the fonts on your system. The Font property controls the appearance of a font. Click on the Font property and then the ![...] symbol at the right, or just double-click the Font property. Either way will display a Font dialog box, as in Figure 5.16.

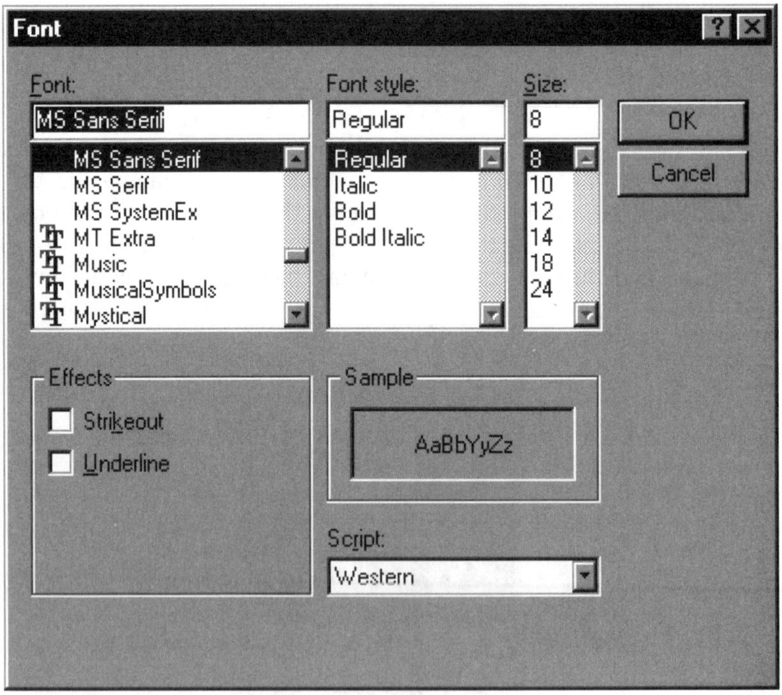

Figure 5.16

When using fonts in an application which is going to be used on a computer other than your own, make sure you only use fonts which everyone will have on their system, such as Arial, Times New Roman and MS Sans Serif.

Position

The position of a control is controlled by four properties: Top, Left, Height and Width. These are measured from the top left-hand corner of the form. The unit of measure is a twip which is one-twentieth of a point. It might be easier to think of it in terms of there being 567 twips to 1 centimetre. Values for these properties are set automatically as the control is created. If you move the control the values will also be changed automatically.

Task 5.2   Labels and more labels!

Start a new project with a blank form. Place several label controls on the form, and change their size, color, borders and the text they display. An example is shown in Figure 5.17.

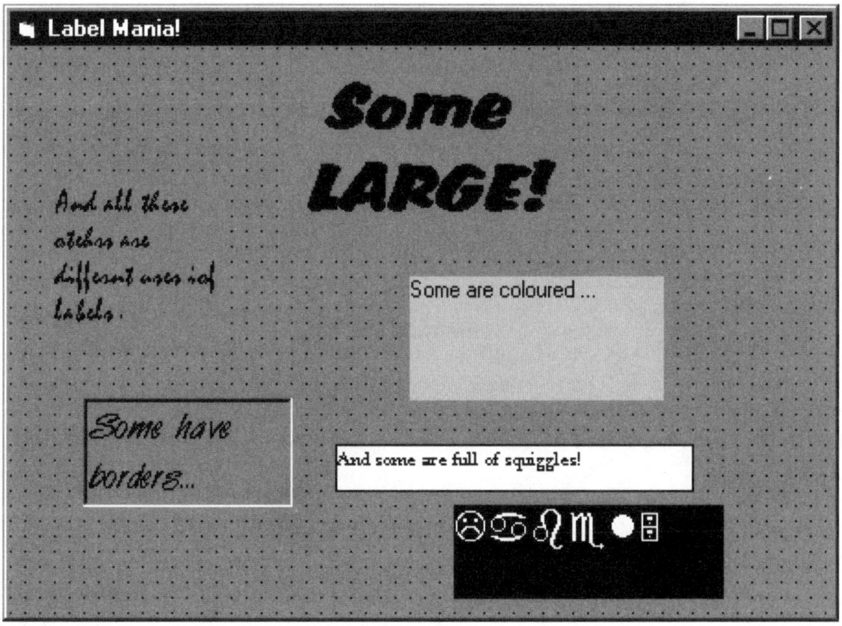

Figure 5.17

Text boxes

Label controls let you display messages to the user. Text boxes can also do this but are much more versatile as information can be typed into a text box. They are used for *input* of information.

The text box is drawn on the form in the normal way. Try this out by drawing a text box.

Run the program to see how a text box works in an application. Press F5 to run the project. Your screen should be similar to Figure 5.18.

Figure 5.18

You will see a cursor in the text box. Try editing and changing the text in the text box, as in Figure 5.19.

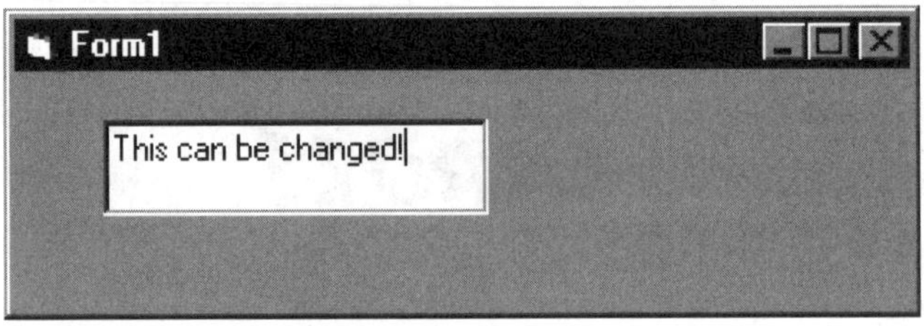

Figure 5.19

This shows the main difference between the label and the text box: the text in a text box can be modified by the user. The text in a label can only be changed by the program.

Naming the text box

Visual Basic names the text box Text1. This can be changed using the (Name) property. It is a good idea to name the control to reflect its use. The standard prefix for text boxes is txt. There is more information on naming controls later in this chapter.

Changing the text in a text box

The text displayed in the text box is not set using the Caption property (it doesn't have one). Instead, the Text property is used as shown in Figure 5.20.

```
Properties - Text1                    ⌧
─────────────────────────────────────
Text1  TextBox                        ▾
─────────────────────────────────────
 Alphabetic │ Categorized │
─────────────────────────────────────
Tag                              │  ▲
Text              │Text1         │
ToolTipText       │              │  ▾
─────────────────────────────────────
Text
Returns/sets the text contained in the control.
```

Figure 5.20

By default, the text property is set to the same value as the (Name) property. This displays in the text box when it is run. This can be annoying for the user as it has to be deleted before new text can be entered. You can avoid this by blanking out the Text property so you have an empty box ready for user input.

The text property always contains the contents of the text box. If the user types in the text box, the text property will change. This makes it possible to find out what has been typed from within your program.

Borders, colors, fonts and position are set in the same way as for labels.

Displaying more than one line of text

A text box normally holds a single line of text. When the box is full it scrolls to the right to accept more text. It often looks better to display the text on several lines in the text box. This is done by setting the MultiLine property. If MultiLine is set to True, when the right of the box is reached it wraps back to the left on the next line. Figure 5.21 shows the effect of the MultiLine property.

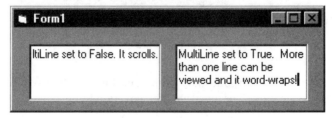

Figure 5.21

Command buttons

This tool draws Windows style command buttons on your form. Command Buttons are used to perform actions, for example OK and Cancel.

A Command Button is placed on a form in the usual way, as shown in Figure 5.22.

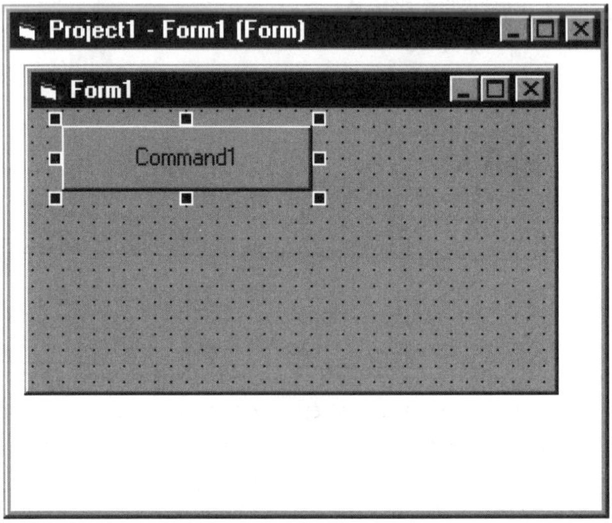

Figure 5.22

Buttons in Windows normally become sunken when clicked. This only happens when the program is running. Press F5 to run the program and then try clicking on the button. A sample result is shown in Figure 5.23.

Figure 5.23

At the moment, you cannot make command buttons do anything. You have to write code to do this. The next chapter covers adding code so that buttons work.

Naming command buttons

This is done as before using the (Name) property. The standard prefix for a button is cmd. As before, you should use meaningful names: for example, cmdStart, cmdStop.

Changing the caption

The Caption property determines what is displayed on the button. It defaults to the name but can be changed.

Adding a ToolTip

A ToolTip is a small yellow instruction box which pops up when the mouse pointer stays over an object for a short length of time. You will have noticed them in Visual Basic itself. An example is shown in Figure 5.24.

Figure 5.24

You can add ToolTips to any Visual Basic object. Set the ToolTipText property to the text you want displayed in the box. Now run your project and the ToolTip will work. No special programming is required.

Changing the appearance of a button

Apart from changing the size of the button, little can be done to change the appearance. Although there is a background color property and an appearance property, these have no effect as buttons use the standard Windows desktop settings.

The font can be changed as before, using the Font property.

De-activating the button

The Enabled property affects whether or not the button can be used. If Enabled is True, it works normally, as above. If Enabled is False, the button is greyed out and cannot be clicked, as shown in Figure 5.25.

Figure 5.25

Another way of stopping the button from being used is to set its Visible property to False. This makes it disappear from the form.

> When Visible is False the button can still be seen at design time, but does not appear at run time.

Focus

An object has the *focus* when it is active. This could be when the insertion point is in a text box, or when a dotted border is around a command button.

When a control has the focus, all keys pressed on the keyboard are processed by that control. For example, if a text box has the focus, then when you type, the text appears in the text box. If a command button has the focus, only the Enter key does anything. The Enter key simulates a mouse click.

You can change the control which has the focus either by using the mouse to click on a different object, or by using the Tab key. The Tab key cycles through all the controls on the form in a pre-defined order, giving each one the focus in turn. The order in which this happens is determined by the TabIndex property. The first control placed on the form has a TabIndex of zero. As each control is drawn it is given the next number. If you wish a particular control to always have focus when the form is loaded this can be done by setting the TabIndex property of that control to zero. It can also be done from within the code as you will see in the next chapter.

Task 5.3

- Draw three command buttons captioned First, Second and Third.
- Draw three text boxes with Text set to First, Second and Third.
- Investigate the effect of using the Tab key to flick the focus between them.
- See when it is possible to type in each text box.
- Set the TabIndex property so the focus always starts in text box Third.

Naming conventions

By now you will have discovered that Visual Basic gives each new control a name which is made up of the type of control plus a number. For example, command buttons would be called Command1, Command2 and so on. These names are not very descriptive, and so it is usual and highly recommended to change them. This becomes particularly important if you are going to create projects of any size. When you have several forms and large numbers of controls it becomes very difficult to keep track of them all.

To distinguish one type of control from another, a set of standard prefixes is usually used. These are shorter than the Visual Basic default names.

The prefixes are as below:

Control	Prefix
Form	frm
Label	lbl
Text Box	txt
Command Button	cmd
Option Button	opt
Check Box	chk
List Box	lst
Combo Box	cbo
Shape	shp
Line	lin
Timer	tmr
Image	img
Picture	pic
Horizontal Scroll Bar	hsb
Vertical Scroll Bar	vsb

The second part of the name should be something which explains what the control does. For example, an OK command button would be called cmdOK, a size label could be lblSize and a text box for the number of turns could be txtNoTurns.

No spaces are allowed in names, so often capital letters are used to denote the start of a new word.

Task 5.4   Hello World!

Start a new project. Name the form frmWorld and set its caption.

Draw a text box control. Give it a white background and change its text to say Hello World! Name the text box txtWorld.

Place command buttons saying: Normal, Bold, Visible, Invisible, Small, Medium, Large. Remember to change the default names of the buttons to more meaningful names using the standard naming conventions. For example, change Command1 to cmdStyleNormal.

Add labels above the sets of buttons to group them together according to type. For example, put a Size label above the set of buttons Small, Medium and Large.

An example is shown in Figure 5.26.

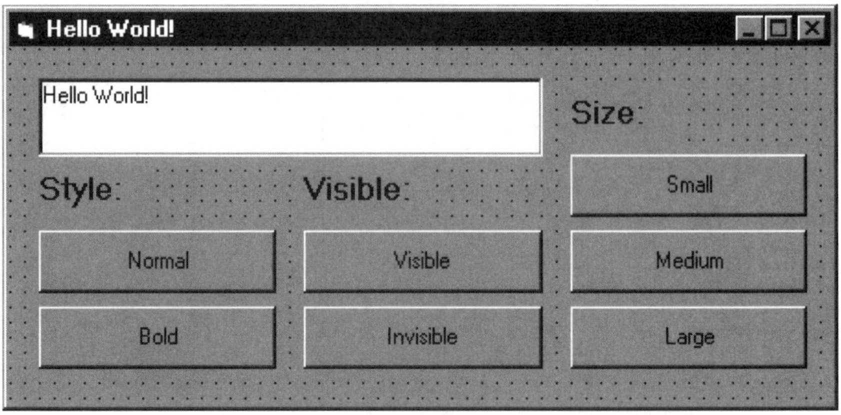

Figure 5.26

Try running the project (press F5) and you should be able to type in the text box and change the text displayed. The buttons are useless at the moment; they can be pressed, but need code attached to them before they can perform any useful function.

Make sure you save this project. You will add code to it in Chapter 6 and make it work.

Summary

In this chapter you have:

- seen how to add controls to a form
- used the label control to add text to a form
- used text boxes to get user input
- used command buttons
- learnt about focus and naming conventions.

Adding code

So far you have created controls and changed their properties. To create applications which interact with the user, code must be added. This chapter introduces the concepts of writing code. The first (and easiest) code is to change the properties of a control while the program is running. This is the main topic of this chapter.

What is code?

Code is a series of instructions which the computer works through in order. These may tell it to display something, change a property or add together a list of numbers. By using code, you can add functionality to an otherwise useless application consisting of solely controls on a form.

In standard programming languages, the computer starts at the top of a list of instructions, and continues processing until it comes to the end. This gives the user very little scope to interact with the program. This is how most DOS programming languages work. Windows languages are very different because the Windows environment gives the user control of what they would like to do and when. Therefore a straightforward "step-through lines of code" approach does not work. Visual Basic uses a form of the BASIC language, but it is different in many ways to other types of BASIC. In Visual Basic most of the code is attached to the form or to controls on the form. The code is run as a response to actions initiated by the user: the events. Visual Basic is an event driven language.

Events

An event is an action which occurs when the user does something. The user may click on a button, type some text, maximize the window or move the mouse. All of these events can have code attached to them. When the event occurs, for example the user clicks on a button, the code associated with that button click is run. This could, for example, change the color of a shape.

In general, the code needed to process an event consists of a few commands which carry out the required tasks and hand control back to the user as quickly as possible.

The code window

The code window is not visible when you start a new project or open an existing one. The code window is opened by double-clicking the form or any control on the form. You may have seen this already if you double-clicked by mistake at any of the earlier points.

Task 6.1 Exploring the code window

- Start a new project.
- Draw a command button on the form.
- Double-click on the button you have created.

This will give you the code window, as shown in Figure 6.1.

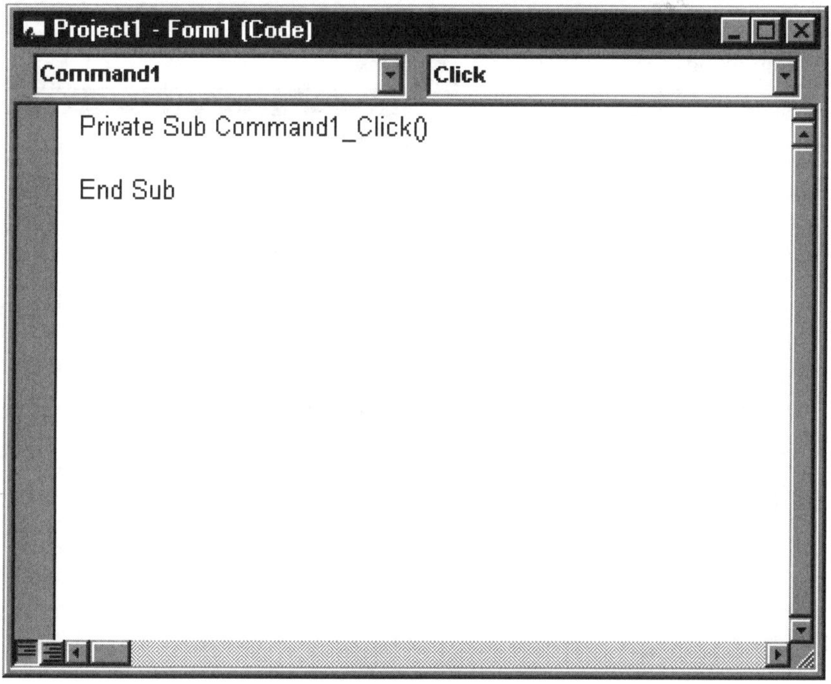

```
Project1 - Form1 (Code)

Command1            ▼    Click                ▼

    Private Sub Command1_Click()

    End Sub
```

Figure 6.1

The left hand box at the top of the window is the Object box – it shows which object the code window relates to.

- Click on the down arrow at the right of the object box. This will give you a list of objects, as shown in Figure 6.2.

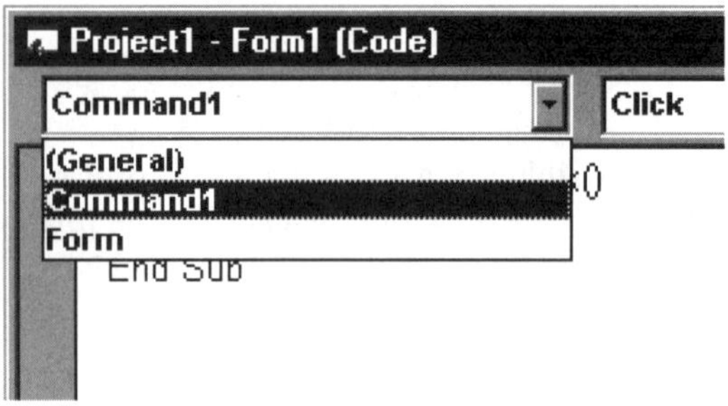

Figure 6.2

This list contains all the controls you have created, plus the form object. Also there is an object called (General) which contains code used by more than one control. This will be covered later in Chapter 17.

- Now click on the arrow of the right-hand (Procedure) box at the right of the window. This will display a list as in Figure 6.3.

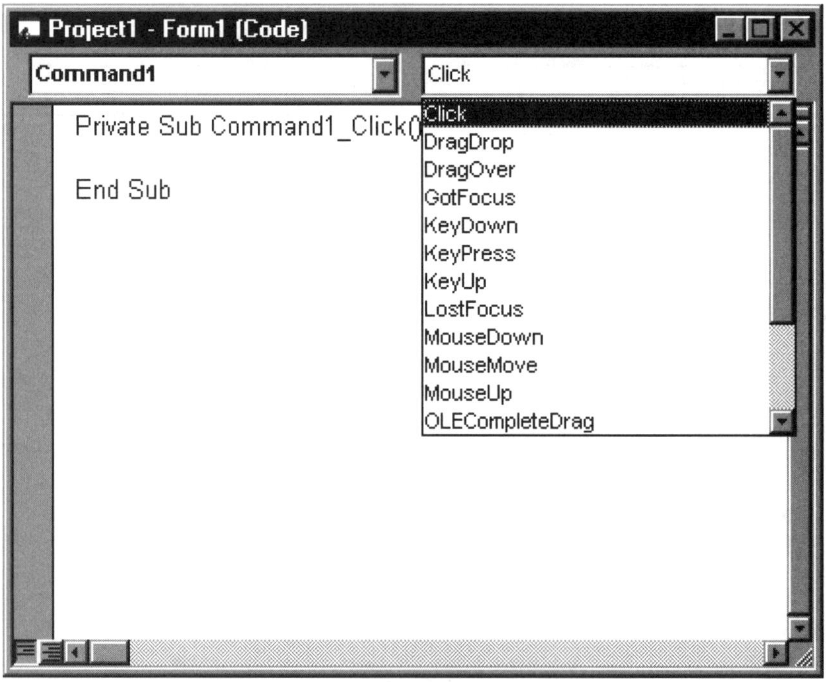

Figure 6.3

This is a list of all the different events to which you can attach code. For the Command1 control, the default event is the Click event. Any code that is written in the Click procedure will be run when the user clicks on the command button.

Code can be written for any of the events in the procedure list. The control will only respond to events for which code has been written. In practice, only a small number of the possible events are coded. Other event procedures which are used frequently include:

- MouseMove – the user moves the mouse over the object
- KeyPress – the user presses a key and the object is currently selected
- DoubleClick – the user double-clicks the object
- Load – the form is loaded

Writing code

The central portion of the code window, as shown in Figure 6.3, is where you type the instructions for the computer to process. The top line reads:

```
Private Sub Command1_Click ()
```

All code is written in subroutines. Every subroutine starts with the name of the subroutine. This is made up of Sub then the name of the object and the name of the event being coded. Private indicates that the subroutine is available for the current form. The subroutine ends with the End Sub line. The example shown is saying that any code written between the Sub line and the End Sub line will only be processed when a Click event occurs on the Command1 Object.

All procedures follow this rule. The general case is

```
Private Sub Object_Event()
```

Changing properties

The simplest use of code is to change properties at run-time as a result of an event. Any properties can be changed. A property for a particular object is referred to by

```
object.property
```

For example, the text written on a command button could be accessed by

```
Command1.Caption
```

Visual Basic 5 has intelligent code which means as soon as you type the full stop a list of properties appears. You can select from the list or carry on typing.

To change a property, the equals sign (=) is used. This changes the property of the object from its current value and gives it a new value. It makes the property equal to the new value.

Intelligent code will also help you here. Some properties will show you a list of valid options.

Examples:

Command	Result
Command1.Caption="New Text"	Caption of a command button Command1 set to New Text
txtWorld.Visible=True	makes the txtWorld text box visible
lblName.Font.Bold=True	displays the text in lblName in Bold type

The quotation marks ("") around "New Text" are needed to tell the computer that any characters inside the quotation marks should be treated as text, and not processed as commands.

Using commands

A command is a line of code which performs an action. The BASIC language has a number of commands. Some commands are simple commands, like Beep; some are more complicated requiring more code. You will meet many of these as you work through later chapters. The Visual Basic built-in help gives details of all commands and their syntax.

To insert a command, you type the command into the code window in the place where the action is to take place.

Beep! Visual Basic does not have to be silent! It can cope with many different sounds. The simplest way of producing a sound is to use the Beep command.

The Beep command can be activated on a click of a command button or when the form is loaded. The code for this is as shown in Figure 6.4.

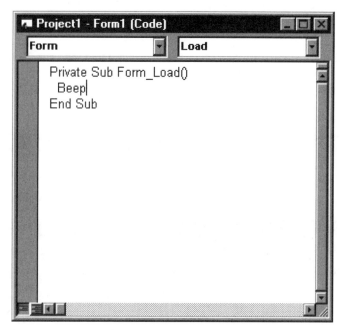

```
Project1 - Form1 (Code)

Form                    Load

    Private Sub Form_Load()
     Beep|
    End Sub
```

Figure 6.4

Task 6.2   Beep!

On a new form, place a command button, labelled Beep. Add the Beep command to the Click event for this button. Then run and test the program.

The sound which the computer produces when it meets a Beep command depends on whether or not you have a sound card. If you do not have a sound card, it will be a standard short beep from the speaker. With a sound card, you can choose the sound it produces from the Control Panel.

Ending the program   The End command closes down your project and stops it running. The End command can be attached to an event, frequently the Click event of a Close or Quit button. If Visual Basic is running, End returns to the design environment.

This task uses the form created in the last chapter. Open the Hello World project. If you did not work through the task in the last chapter, create a form similar to that shown in Figure 6.5.

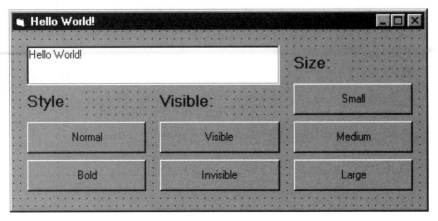

Figure 6.5

In the last chapter, you designed the form. Now you need to add code to the Click events on the buttons to change the properties of the text box control. Use the syntax given above (object.property = new value) and the examples to add code to the Click event for each of the command buttons.

Note that the Font property is different from most properties because it has sub-divisions.

• To change the styles use

txtWorld.Font.Bold=True or False

• To change the font name use

txtWorld.Font.Name="Arial" or "Times New Roman"

• The font name must be in quotation marks to tell the computer it is text. To change the size, use

txtWorld.Font.Size=8 or 12 or 18

for Small, Medium and Large respectively.
• Add an Exit button, and add code to it to close the application.
• An example of the code for the Normal style button is shown in Figure 6.6.

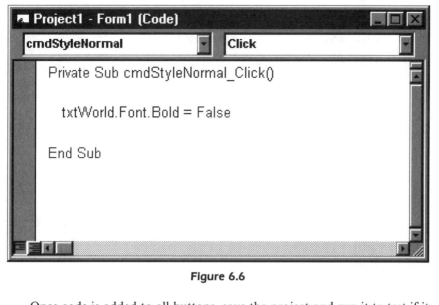

Figure 6.6

Once code is added to all buttons, save the project and run it to test if it works. If it doesn't, you will need to check your lines of code.

Setting focus

You can use code to set the currently selected object on the screen by changing the focus. Refer back to Chapter 5 for more information about focus.
Example:

Text1.SetFocus

gives focus to the Text1 text box. This puts the cursor in Text1 and makes it easier to edit the contents.

Using help when programming

Visual Basic has an extensive built-in help system which is particularly useful when programming. Whenever you are unsure of how a command or a property works, you can type the property name, place the cursor in the word and press F1. Visual Basic will display the help screens associated with that topic.

In Figure 6.7, the cursor is in the word Visible. If you press F1, the help screen is displayed as in Figure 6.8.

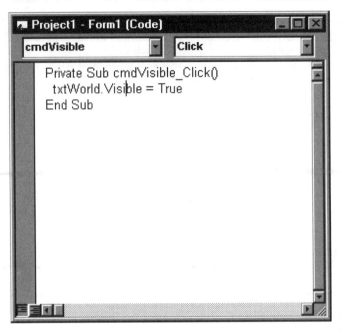

Figure 6.7

Visual Basic Reference

Help Topics   Back   Options

Visible Property

See Also   Example   Applies To   Specifics

Returns or sets a value indicating whether an object is visible or hidden.

Syntax

object.**Visible** [= *boolean*]

The **Visible** property syntax has these parts:

Part	Description
object	An object expression that evaluates to an object in the Applies To list.
boolean	A Boolean expression specifying whether the object is visible or hidden.

Settings

The settings for *boolean* are:

Setting	Description
True	(Default) Object is visible.
False	Object is hidden.

Remarks

To hide an object at startup, set the **Visible** property to **False** at design time. Setting this property in code enables you to hide and later redisplay a control at run time in response to a particular event.

Note   Using the **Show** or **Hide** method on a form is the same as setting the form's **Visible** property in code to **True** or **False**, respectively.

Figure 6.8

The help screen is very comprehensive, but you will often find that help screens contain too much information and can be confusing. At the top of the screen there is usually an Example of the use of the property or command. Click on this and it gives a sample from a program showing how Visible may be used.

Summary

In this chapter you have:

- learnt about code
- added code to change properties
- used some simple Visual Basic commands
- learned how to exit an application
- set focus from code
- used context-sensitive help while programming.

7 Increasing control

Chapter 5 explored the basic controls, labels, text boxes and command buttons, which you will use in just about every application you create. As you know, Visual Basic has many more controls. This chapter introduces more controls and increases your skills in creating and using them.

Check boxes

A check box is used to get input from the user. A check box can be checked or unchecked so it is a very good way of allowing users to make yes/no choices.

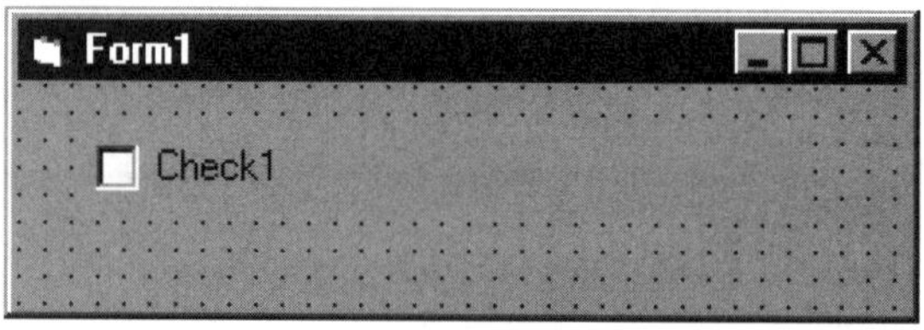

![Form1 window containing a check box labelled Check1]

Figure 7.1

The text displayed next to the check box is controlled by the Caption property.

When drawn, a check box is initially unchecked, as shown in Figure 7.1. It becomes checked when the user clicks in the box. A check box can also be switched on by setting the Value property. The three Values are shown in Figure 7.2.

The *Greyed* tick is used to show when an option is neither on nor off. You may have seen grey ticks used in Windows setup programs to show part of the application is to be installed. A grey tick is not the same as the Enabled property set to False which greys out a control and it cannot be used. A greyed tick can still be used.

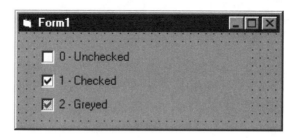

Figure 7.2

— **Task 7.1 Check boxes** —

Draw three check box controls as in Figure 7.2 on a form and investigate how they change when clicked. Notice the sequence which the grey check box follows.

The main event for a check box is the Click event. This occurs whenever the user changes the state of the check box (it can also occur when the state of the check box is changed by pressing Enter). The state of the check box is given by the Value property.

Option buttons

Option buttons are always used in groups. Only one of the buttons in the group can be on at one time. This lets the user select exclusively one option from a list. Figure 7.3 shows three option buttons and what happens when they are clicked.

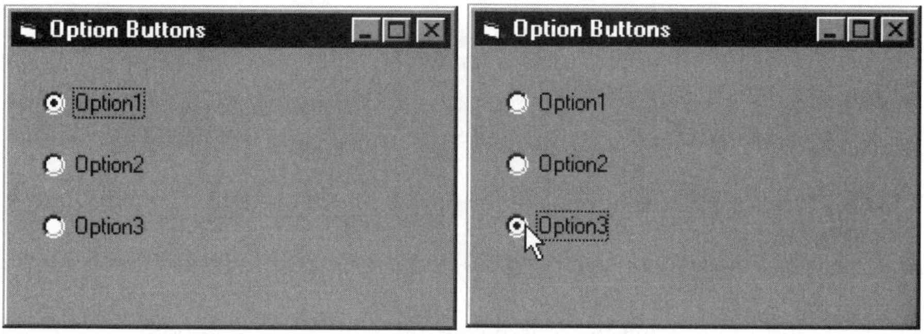

Figure 7.3

Option buttons are sometimes called radio buttons because they are similar to tuning buttons on old radios. You press one, and the previously selected one pops back out.

Task 7.2   Option buttons

Add a set of option buttons to the form created above, and investigate the effect of clicking them. Notice that when you click one, the previously selected option is automatically switched off.

The uses of option buttons include things like selecting gender (M or F) or titles (Mr, Mrs, Ms, etc.) from a group, or selecting age from a group of ages (0–9, 10–19, 20–39, etc.).

The state of an option button is accessed through the Value property. Unlike the check box, it has only two states: On (True) and Off (False).

The main difference between option buttons and check boxes is that only one option button in the group can be selected, whereas each check box can either be on or off, so allowing multiple selections.

It is easier to write code for an option button than for a check box. This is because if the user clicks on an option button, it means it has to be selected, and can be the only one that is selected.

Task 7.3   Good-day!

- Create a form with three label controls on it. Set their Captions to Good Morning, Good Afternoon and Good Night respectively. Set all their Visible properties to false and position them on top of each other on the form.
- Create a set of three option buttons and caption them 7am–midday, midday–5pm, and 5pm–7am respectively.

Remember to set their names to something more memorable. opt is the usual prefix for option buttons.

- Add code to the click events of the option buttons so that the appropriate label shows.
- Run the application. Try the different options and see if the correct label is displayed.

  Remember to switch the other labels off again.

  Figure 7.4 shows the three different states when it is running.

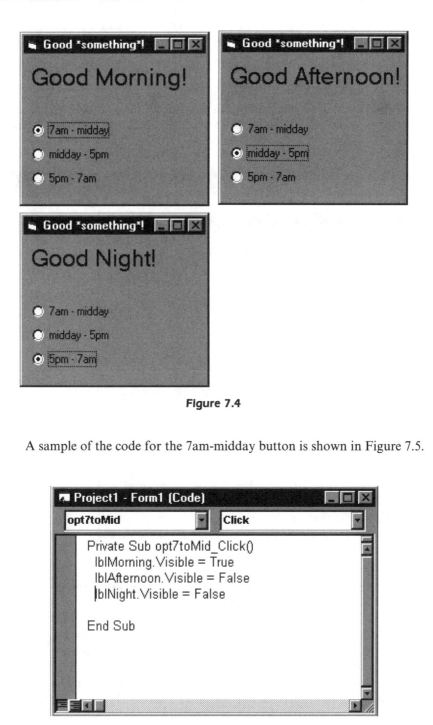

Figure 7.4

A sample of the code for the 7am-midday button is shown in Figure 7.5.

```
Private Sub opt7toMid_Click()
    lblMorning.Visible = True
    lblAfternoon.Visible = False
    lblNight.Visible = False

End Sub
```

Figure 7.5

List boxes

A list box presents the user with a list of options. Any of the options can be selected from the list. A list box makes it easier for users to enter common items as it reduces typing and therefore avoids typing errors.

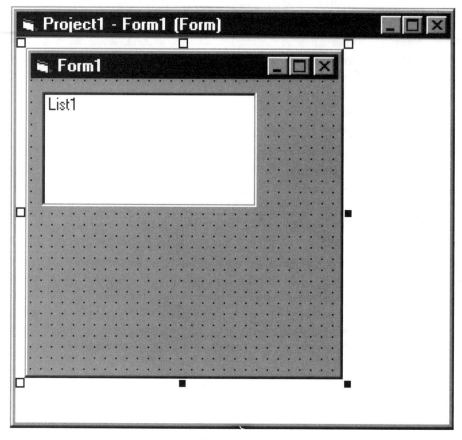

Figure 7.6

The list box is similar to using a set of option buttons: the user is given a choice of options and chooses one of them. The advantage of a list box is that it takes up less space on the form so the form looks less cluttered. A list box is much better if there are a large number of options. You do not have to make the list box large enough to show all the options at once; if the list box is not large enough Visual Basic will automatically add scroll bars to the list box.

Initially, a list box is empty, as in Figure 7.6. The text displayed in a list box is the (Name) property. It has no Caption property, as it contains many text items, not just one.

There are two ways of filling a list box:

- The data can be typed at design time, giving a fixed list of options
- The data can be added and changed at run-time.

Setting up the list at design time

The List property of the control lets you enter a set of options to appear in the list box.

Select the List property and use the down arrow at the right. This will give you an empty box with a cursor in it, as in Figure 7.7.

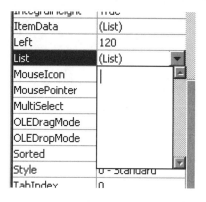

Figure 7.7

This box is used to enter the options for the list. Do not press Enter after each option or the box will close. Instead, hold down Ctrl while pressing Enter to enter the next option. Repeat for each of the options. Figure 7.8 shows multiple entries in the List property.

IntegralHeight	True
ItemData	(List)
Left	120
List	(List)
MouseIcon	Mr
MousePointer	Mrs
MultiSelect	Miss
	Ms
OLEDragMode	Dr
OLEDropMode	Other
Sorted	
Style	0 - Standard
TabIndex	0

Figure 7.8

When all the options have been entered, press Enter to close the property box. The list values will now be displayed in the list box, as in Figure 7.9.

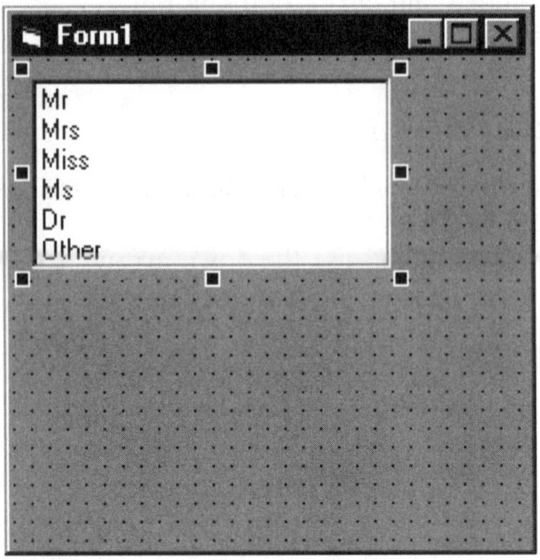

Figure 7.9

Task 7.4   List boxes

Create a List box control and enter a list of options.
Run the program and see how the options can be selected, both with the mouse and with the keys.

Setting up the list at run time

If the values are known when you create the form and do not change, it is easier to set them up in the List property at design time. If options will change at run-time, code is required.

Start with the empty list control as above. This time, items are only added to the list when the program is running. This is done using the *AddItem method*. A method performs an action on an object. The AddItem method adds an item to the list-box object List1. The syntax is:

List1.AddItem "value1"

This tells the computer to add the text **Value1** to the list box List1.

The items can be added to the list box at any time they are required. If the list box is required to display its options as soon as the program is run the AddItem commands need to be placed at the start of the application. This is achieved by placing them in the Load event of the Form. Not surprisingly, this event happens when the form is loaded! If the list box starts life as an empty box without any values, you could have a command button which displays the values when clicked. In this case, the AddItem commands would be placed in the Click event of the command button.

___ Task 7.5   Adding to a list _____

Set up a form which contains a list box, a text box and a command button marked Add. An example is shown in Figure 7.10.

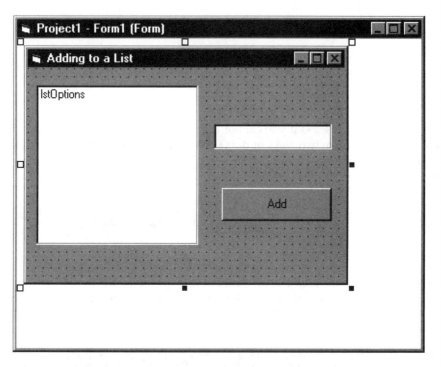

Figure 7.10

Insert code in the click event of the Add button to add the text from the text box to the list box.

Run the program and try typing in the text box and clicking on Add. This should enable items to be added to the list box.

If you need some help, an example of the code is shown in Figure 7.11.

Try amending the program so that the text box is automatically emptied when the Add button is clicked. This makes it easier for the user to add another option to the list.

See if you can add code to give focus to the text box ready for the next item. Remember you can always check the help screens.

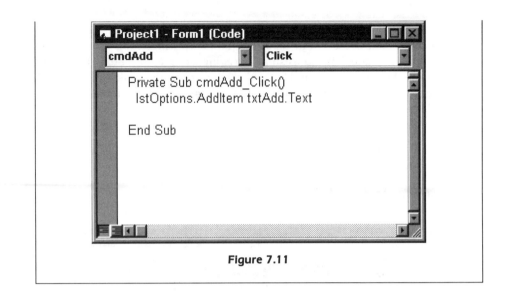

Figure 7.11

Finding out which option is selected

A list of options is useless if you cannot tell which option the user has selected. In Visual Basic there are two ways of doing this: you can find out the number of the option which has been selected or the actual text.

The ListIndex property is the number of the option in the list.

The top option in the list is 0, the second is 1 and so on.

The Text property of a list control returns the text of the currently selected option. This is more useful than the ListIndex property which just returns the position in the list. For instance, in the list box shown in Figure 7.12, Text would be set to "Alabama". ListIndex would be 4.

Figure 7.12

Sorting a list box

Normally a list box displays the items in the order that they were entered. Visual Basic can automatically sort the contents of list boxes. The Sorted property can either be True or False. If it is False (the default), then the options appear in the list box in the order in which they were entered. If Sorted is True, they are automatically sorted into alphabetical order. An example is shown in Figure 7.13.

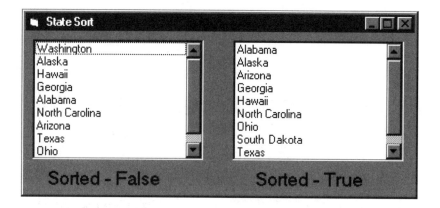

Figure 7.13

Combo boxes

A combo box is similar to a list box except that usually only the selected item is displayed. The other choices can be displayed by clicking on the arrow. A combo box therefore needs less space on the form and is used instead of a list box where space is limited.

As for a list box, items can either be entered at design time using the List property or at run-time using the AddItem method.

Styles of combo box

Style Properties are listed overleaf and examples of the different styles of combo box are shown in Figure 7.14.

Style Property	Description
0 – Dropdown Combo	lets the user choose from the list by using the arrow and also accepts text which is not on the list.
1 – Simple Combo	has no arrow, but instead the list is displayed all the time. It is similar to a list box, but also accepts text which is not on the list. The size of the control must be big enough to include both the top line and also the selection list.
2 – Dropdown List Box	looks like a Dropdown Combo box, but only lets you select from the items in the list.

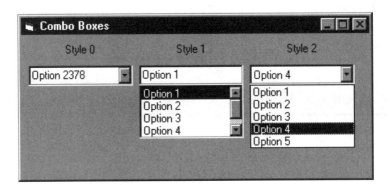

Figure 7.14

Task 7.6   Combo boxes

Start a new project and add three combo boxes. Add about five options to each box. Set the Style property of each Combo box to 0, 1 and 2 respectively.

Run the project, and try both choosing from the list and typing your own options which are not included in the list.

Scroll bars

Visual Basic has two scroll bar controls: horizontal and vertical. The scroll bar is a graphical way of selecting values within a pre-set range. It could be used to set speeds, quantities or sizes. Figure 7.15 shows some sample scroll bar controls. As you can see, a variety of shapes and sizes can be created.

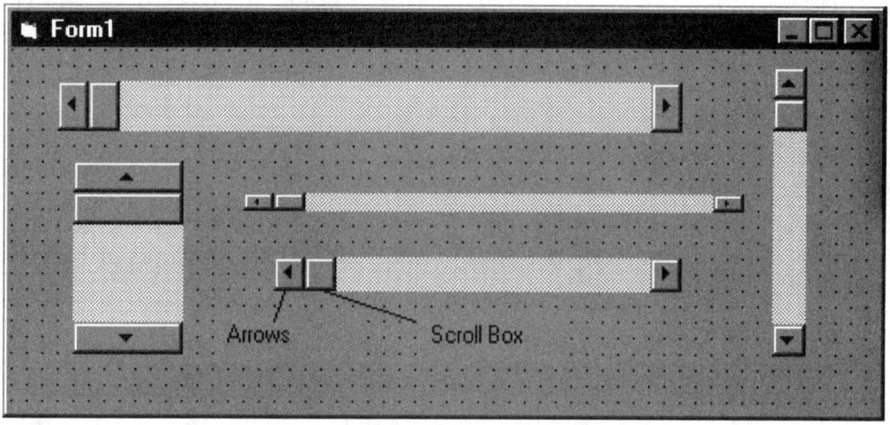

Figure 7.15

The scroll bar is able to return many values within the range. The range and the values which are possible are set by properties of the control.

Property	Description
Min	The minimum value the scroll bar should return. This will be the value returned when the scroll box is at the top or left hand end of the bar.
Max	The maximum value the scroll bar should return. This will be the value returned when the scroll box is at the bottom or right hand end of the bar.
SmallChange	This is by how much the scroll box should move when the arrows at the ends of the bar are clicked.
LargeChange	This is by how much the scroll box should move if the user clicks in the bar. This should be larger than SmallChange because the box should move more rapidly: clicking in the bar is for large adjustments; clicking on the arrows is for fine adjustments. In Windows 95, the ratio of LargeChange to the overall range also affects the size of the scroll box. The larger the LargeChange, the greater is the proportion of the scroll bar taken up by the scroll box.

The current position of the scroll box is returned by the Value property. This will always be between the Min and Max values.

Task 7.7 Scrolling

Start a new project. Place a label control in the top left of the screen, and two scroll bars along the bottom and right of the screen, as in Figure 7.16.

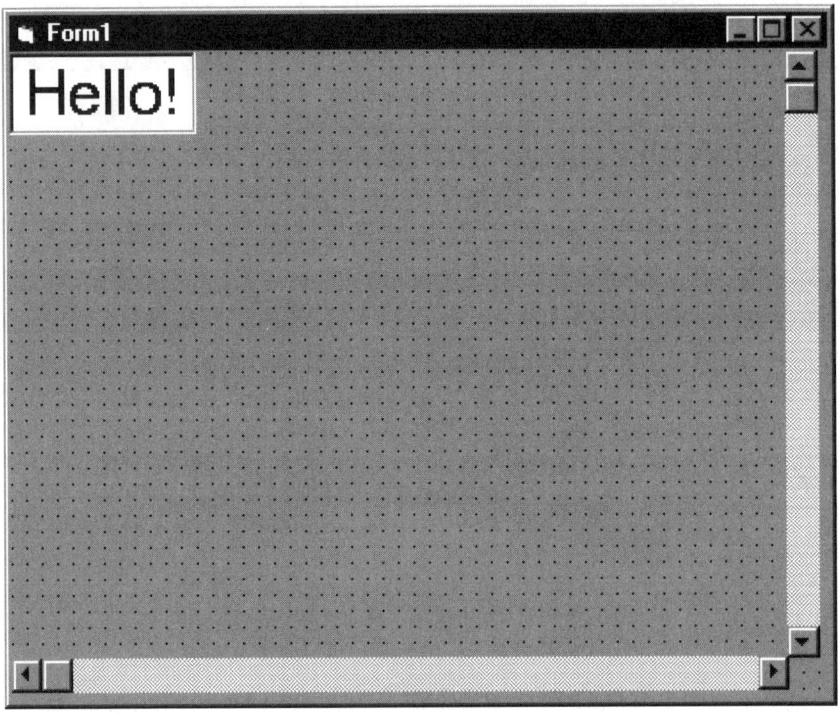

Figure 7.16

Set the Max property of the bottom scroll bar to the width of the form (this can be found by looking at the Width property of the form, or by looking at the dimensions boxes at the right-hand side of the toolbar).

Set the Max property of the right-hand scroll bar to the height of the form.

Set the small and large change properties to reasonable values, about a tenth of the Max for LargeChange and about a hundredth of the Max for SmallChange.

Add code to the Change events of the scroll boxes so that when the scroll bars are moved, the position of the label moves with them. This is done by changing the Top and Left properties of the label to the values given by the scroll bars.

Run and test the program.

Timer control

A timer control is a special control which generates an event (the Timer event) at regular intervals. It is useful for animating graphics where an object moves at a steady rate, or the color changes every second. A timer control is different from controls looked at so far because it does not appear on the screen at run time. At design time the timer control appears as an icon as shown in Figure 7.17. It does not matter where this icon is placed. It can be placed in a corner out of the way of the controls on the form.

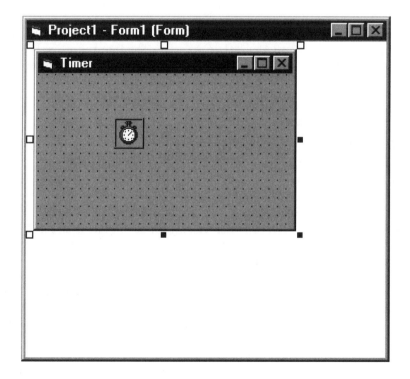

Figure 7.17

```
Properties - Timer1                    [x]
Timer1  Timer                           [v]
 Alphabetic | Categorized
 (Name)       Timer1
 Enabled      True
 Index
 Interval     0
 Left         1080
 Tag
 Top          600


 Interval
 Returns/sets the number of milliseconds between
 calls to a Timer control's Timer event.
```

Figure 7.18

The properties of the Timer Control are shown in Figure 7.18. It has very few properties because it has no physical appearance. The Interval property specifies the time between each event. It is measured in milliseconds, so 1000 gives a pause of one second. The Enabled property switches the timer on or off.

Task 7.8   Up, up and away!

Start a new project.

Set up a long thin form which contains a label, a timer, two option buttons marked On and Off, a Reset command button and a scroll bar to regulate the speed, as in Figure 7.19.

- Add code to the timer event so that the label moves up the screen by 100 twips (the standard screen measurement) for each timer event.
- Set the range of the scroll bar between 0 and 200. When the scroll bar is changed, the interval property of the Timer should be changed.
  Remember that the higher the timer interval, the slower the label moves. To reverse the effect of this, the interval can be set to 201 minus the scroll bar value.
- Add code to the On and Off option buttons. When On, Enabled should be true so the label moves.
- Add code to the Reset button to change the Top property of the label to its initial value. (You will need to check the Top property of the label.)
- Run and test the program.

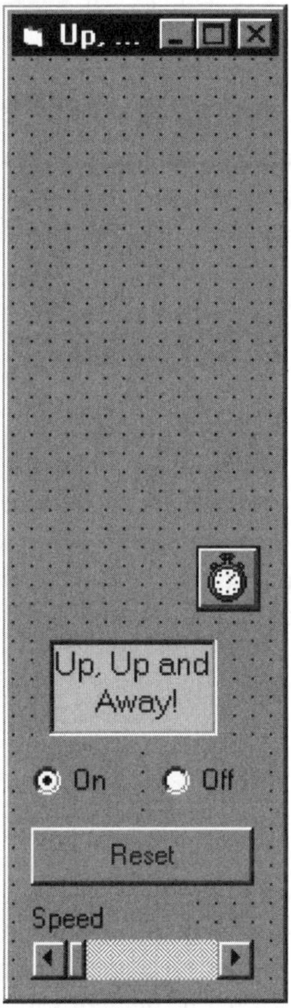

Figure 7.19

Summary

In this chapter you have:

- used check boxes and option buttons
- used list boxes and combo boxes
- entered options to list and combo boxes
- used scroll bar controls
- learnt how to use the timer control.

Doing more with code

So far you have written code which makes changes to the properties of objects on the form when a specific event occurs. A lot can be accomplished with even such simple programming but you are able to do many other things with Visual Basic code. You have probably found that there were things you wanted to do when working through the tasks but did not know how. This chapter aims to provide many of these skills.

Making decisions

One of the most frequent tasks when programming is that you need to test for something being true, then make decisions about what to do based on the result of the test. You only make a cup of tea if the water is boiling. A bill cannot be paid if there are insufficient funds. The general case is that IF something is true THEN an action will take place.

You first have to write the code to test the condition or conditions, then write the code for the response. Visual Basic and other programming languages have a number of ways of writing code for test conditions. The simplest form is the If . . . Then statement or command.

If command

In Visual Basic the command is written as:

If condition Then statements [Else elsestatements]

The command always starts with If. You then have to write the code for the selection conditions. Visual Basic uses the standard operators for creating conditions within your programs.

Operator	Condition
=	equals
>	greater than
> =	greater than or equal to
<	less than
> =	less than or equal to
< >	not equal to

If commands can be used to test the values of properties and variables.

Examples:

If txtName.Enabled=False Then txtName.Enabled=True
tests whether the text box txtName is enabled and ready for input. If it isn't then the text box is enabled. There is no Else part.

If hsbSpeed.Value<200 Then lblMove.Top=lblMove.Top – 10
moves lblMove up the form by 10 twips for scroll bar values less than 200

If x>y Then lblLargest=x Else lblLargest=y
compares 2 numbers x and y and displays the highest number in lblLargest

If condition Then statements [Else elsestatements]

The Else part of the command allows an alternative action to the Then action as in the third example. You do not need to have an Else part; it is optional. This is shown by the square brackets round the Else part of the statement.

___ **Task 8.1 Passwords** _____

- Draw a label and name it lblPassword. Set the caption to "Enter your Password".
- Draw a text box and name it txtPassword. Blank out the text. Set the PasswordChar property to *. This changes the text box so that when text is typed into it, it is not displayed and appears as asterisks.
- Draw a second label and name it lblCorrect, and an OK command button named cmdOK.
- Add a Quit button and write code to make it end the program. Check back in chapter 6 if you have forgotten how to do this.

Figure 8.1 shows a possible layout for your form.

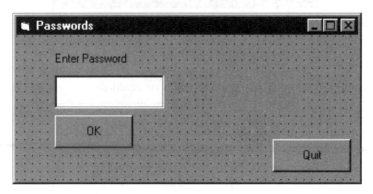

Figure 8.1

Run the program. Type a word into the text box. The text box will display an * for each letter that you type.

Stop the program running.

Write code for the click event of the OK button which will test the word entered against the correct password (you decide what this is!). If the password is correct, set the caption of the label to PROCEED! If it is incorrect, set the caption to STOP! Use the FontSize and FontName properties to fill the label and add impact.

Run the program. Enter a wrong word and then the correct word and see what happens.

Save the project for later use.

Block If command

In Visual Basic the If . . . Then statement can also take another form. This is more versatile as it allows a number of statements to be executed if the condition is true. This is known as the *Block If*. The Else part is optional as before. Each part must start on a new line as shown. The Block If is ended by a line saying End If. This tells Visual Basic that the Then or Else statements have finished.

```
If condition Then
    statements
[Else
    elsestatements]
End If
```

Example:

```
If txtName.Enabled=False Then
    txtName.Enabled=True
    txtName.SetFocus
End If
```

Change the code on the OK button so the text box, OK button and lblPassword are no longer displayed when a correct password is entered. Use a Block If to do this.

    Save the project for later use.

Combining conditions

Quite often you will need to use more than one condition to produce the right test. You might want to check whether both a name and a password have been correctly entered. Conditions can be combined using another set of operators.

Condition	Description
And	both conditions must be true
Or	either condition can be true
Not	condition must not be true

Example:

If txtName <> "" And txtPassword <> "" Then . . ..

This will run the Then statements only if both a name and a password have been entered.

Message boxes

Another common requirement when you are writing programs is to communicate with the user and display information messages. Visual Basic uses the MsgBox statement which produces a standard Windows message box with an OK button. The text displayed in the box can be anything you like.

    A standard MsgBox look like that shown in Figure 8.2. Clicking OK removes the message box from the screen.

Figure 8.2

By now, you will not be surprised to hear that Visual Basic allows you to have very much more sophisticated message boxes than this simple one! The message box can have a title, an icon and extra buttons.

The syntax of the MsgBox statement is:

MsgBox message [,type, title]

where:

message is the text to appear in the box
type determines the buttons and icons available in the message box
title is the text to appear on the title bar of the message box

Type is a number made up of a number for the icon and a number for the message box buttons. The numbers are added together to give the Type value.

Type value	Icon
0	OK button only
1	OK and Cancel
2	Abort, Retry and Ignore
3	Yes, No and Cancel
4	Yes and No
5	Retry and Cancel
16	Stop
32	Question
64	Information

Example:

MsgBox "Are you sure?", 36, "Exit"

gives the message box shown in Figure 8.3.

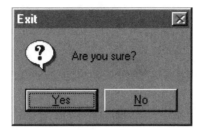

Figure 8.3

Visual Basic version 5 contains Quick information which gives help with the syntax as you are writing your code. Figure 8.4 shows what you will see as you type a MsgBox command.

```
MsgBox(Prompt, [Buttons As VbMsgBoxStyle = vbOKOnly], [Title], [HelpFile], [Context])
As VbMsgBoxResult
```

Figure 8.4

___ **Task 8.3   Passwords again!** _____

Change your password program so the correct password is displayed in a message box if the guess is correct. If an incorrect password is entered display an error message in a message box with a Stop symbol.
    Save the project again.

Select Case statement

Select Case is a decision structure that selects and executes a single block of code from two or more blocks of code. It is a neater way of selecting multiple conditions than using a series of "If . . . Then" statements.
    The code structure:

- starts with Select Case followed by the value being tested
- ends with End Select
- has one or more Case blocks between Select and End Select
- allows code to be written in the Case Else which is executed if none of the other cases are true.

Only one of the Case blocks can be executed.

Example

```
Select Case txtMonth
    Case "Dec", "Jan", "Feb"
        lblSeason="Winter"
    Case "Mar", "Apr", "May"
        lblSeason="Spring"
    Case "Jun", "Jul", "Aug"
        lblSeason="Summer"
    Case "Sep", "Oct", "Nov"
        lblSeason="Autumn"
    Case Else
        MsgBox ("Invalid month", 34, "Error")
End Select
```

This example finds out what text has been entered in the txtMonth text box, selects the appropriate season and displays the result in lblSeason. If anything else is entered an error message is displayed.

Storing information

When you are writing programs you will need to store information so it can be used later in the program. The information could have been input by the user or it could have been calculated within the program. One of the powerful features of programming languages is that they are able to use segments of the memory of the computer as temporary storage areas for such information while the program is running. The area of memory used to store the information is called a *variable*. Once the program is ended, the variable ceases to exist and the information will be lost.

Variables

The program can have many variables all existing at the same time, each holding a different piece of information. The information can be text such as a name, a date or a number or amount. The value contained within a variable can be changed by the program or by input from the user. When this happens the old value is lost. A variable can only hold value at any one time.

A variable is a bit like a property of a control: they can both store information while the program is running. Variables are different in that they are independent of the form or control and cannot be directly changed by the user.

Task 8.4 Temperature convertor

Start a new project.

- Set up a form which has two text boxes on it. Label one Celsius and the other Fahrenheit.
- Add a small command button under each text box with the caption Clear.
- Draw a large command button in between the text boxes labelled Convert.

An example is shown in Figure 8.5.

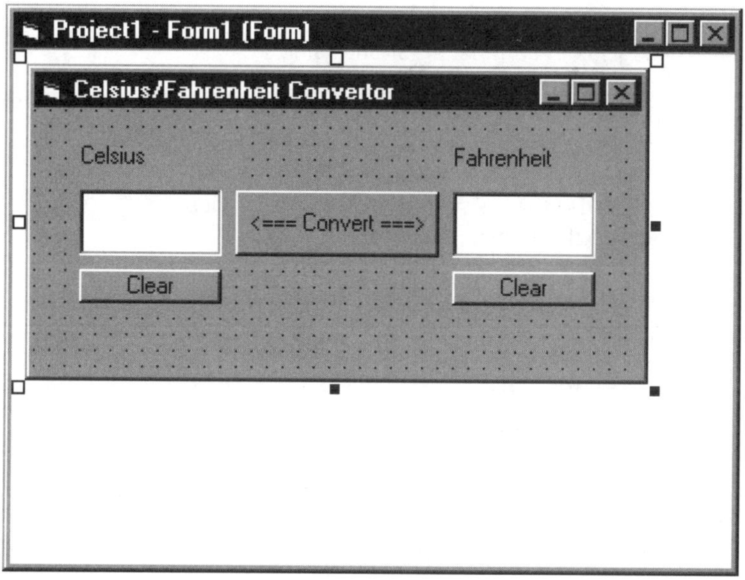

Figure 8.5

Add code to the clear buttons to clear the respective text box. The convert button has to work out which of the boxes are filled and act accordingly.

Neither filled – produce an error
One filled – output the conversion in the other text box
Both filled – produce an error

You can test for the text box being empty using ""

It is good practice to store the value from the text box in a variable, and then apply the conversion to this variable.

If you have forgotten the conversion rules – to convert from Celsius to Fahrenheit: multiply by 9, then divide by 5, then add 32. To convert from Fahrenheit to Celsius: subtract 32, multiply by 5 and then divide by 9.

If you need help, one possible way of doing this is shown in Figure 8.6.

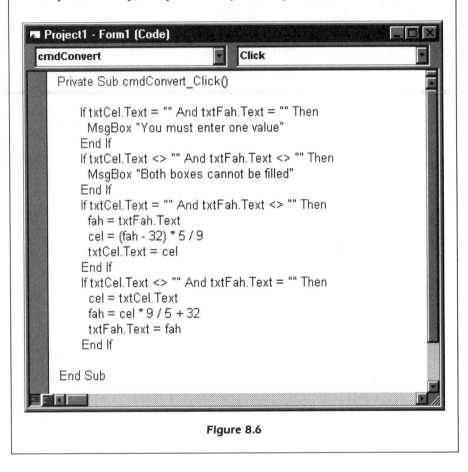

```
Project1 - Form1 (Code)

cmdConvert                          Click

    Private Sub cmdConvert_Click()

        If txtCel.Text = "" And txtFah.Text = "" Then
          MsgBox "You must enter one value"
        End If
        If txtCel.Text <> "" And txtFah.Text <> "" Then
          MsgBox "Both boxes cannot be filled"
        End If
        If txtCel.Text = "" And txtFah.Text <> "" Then
          fah = txtFah.Text
          cel = (fah - 32) * 5 / 9
          txtCel.Text = cel
        End If
        If txtCel.Text <> "" And txtFah.Text = "" Then
          cel = txtCel.Text
          fah = cel * 9 / 5 + 32
          txtFah.Text = fah
        End If

    End Sub
```

Figure 8.6

Declaration of variables

A variable, like a control, is given a name which you can use to access it. Each variable used in the same project must have a different name. Variable names have to follow certain rules – they must start with a letter, cannot contain spaces or full stops and must be shorter than 255 characters. In practice it is very unlikely you would use any names as long as this! Most variable names tend to be short – around 10 characters or less. You also are not allowed to use any reserved words for variable names. A reserved word is a word used by Visual Basic itself such as Print or Date.

In Visual Basic you can set up and use a variable just by putting some information into it.

Example	Description
amount=123.45	puts the value 123.45 into a variable called amount
message="Good Bye"	puts Good Bye into a variable called message

You can also set up a variable by declaring it in the code. This is known as *declaration*. The command used is **Dim** which stands for Dimension.

Dim variablename [As datatype]

You will find out more about data types in the next section.

Scope of variables

You can put a Dim statement anywhere you like in the code. However, it is important that you put the Dim statements in the right place as this determines which parts of the program know about the variable. This is called the *scope* of the variable. Dim statements are usually placed at the top of the procedure where they can easily be located. It is also useful to add a comment to indicate the purpose of the variable.

Where declared	Available
inside a procedure	in that procedure only
(General) (Declarations) section	throughout the form

Data types

You have seen that the main purpose of programs is to manipulate data. There are many different types of data. This includes data input by the user which could be numeric, dates, textual or yes/no choices. It could also be values which have been calculated by the program and stored in a variable.

Here are some types of data:

Type	Example
numeric	1234.56
string	"Hello"
date	01/01/2000
Boolean	True or False, Yes or No
integer	16

In Visual Basic the data can also be a property of a control. Each property has a data type. This may be set by Visual Basic itself; for example, properties such as Visible which can be True or False (Boolean). It may also be determined by the value that you set for the property. For example, Caption is string data type but it can also display numeric values.

Visual Basic variables also have data types. You can decide which type of data you are storing and declare the variable as a specific data type or you can let Visual Basic decide for you. Visual Basic allocates the *variant* data type to any variable you use in a program without previously declaring it. The variant data type is a special data type that can contain any kind of data. Visual Basic works out whether the data being stored is numeric or string data.

Using data types

You may well find that understanding and using the various data types is not easy. When you are finding your way around, you will find it simplest to allow Visual Basic to declare your variables. These will then all be given the variant data type.

Data types often cause problems because they produce errors when your program is run. One of the common error types is a data type mismatch which happens when the data type you have used is different from the one that Visual Basic expects. These errors are resolved by converting to another data type. This is done by a Visual Basic *function* and you will find out about functions in the next chapter.

Constants

A *constant* is a named item that has the same value all the time the program is running. You can create constants and use them anywhere in your code instead of actual values. Constants are useful when a value is used many times throughout a program as it saves typing the value in each time and therefore reduces errors. Another advantage of using a constant is that if the value changes the program only needs to be changed in one place. Constants can contain character strings or numeric values or expressions.

A constant is declared in the (General) (Declarations) section by:

Const Pi As Single=3.142
Const Company="My company name"

___ **Task 8.5   Circle calculator** _____

Start a new project.
    Design a form which will calculate the area of a circle from the radius which is entered by the user. A sample form is shown in Figure 8.7.

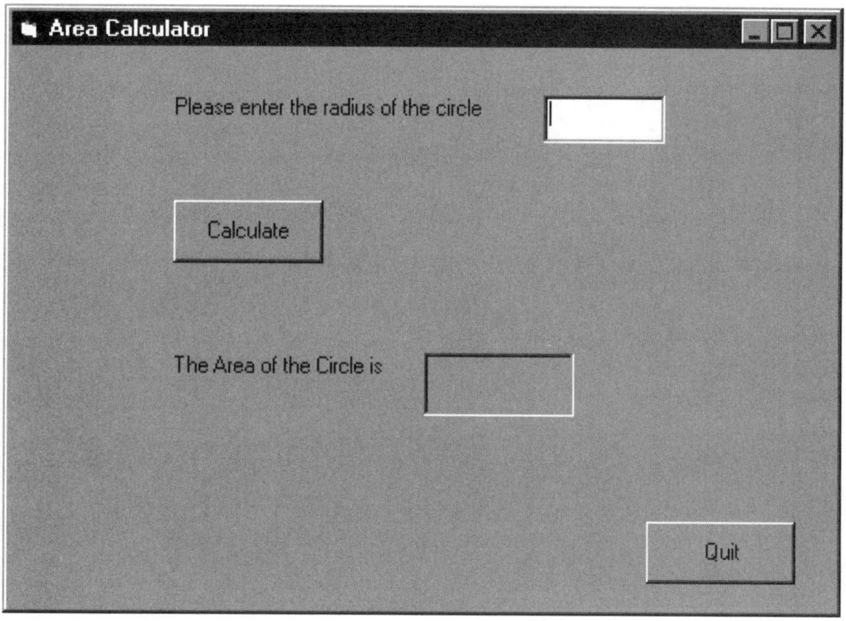

Figure 8.7

Write code to calculate the area of the circle using the formula

Area = π * Radius * Radius

where π is a constant value 3.142

You can also try to make the program calculate the circumference of the circle as well as the area (this is worked out by 2 * π * radius).

Making your code easier to read

Comments

You can, and should, add comments to your code to explain what the code is doing. You might think you will be able to remember but some months or years later it can be very time-consuming to work out what the program is trying to do. Using comments will also help other people to understand your code.

You can add comments or remarks anywhere in the code. Each comment starts with a single apostrophe ('). Comments can be placed on a line on their own or can be placed on the same line after the Visual Basic commands. All the rest of the text on the line after the apostrophe will be ignored.

Examples:

```
'This is a comment
cmdStart.SetFocus    'set focus to Start button
```

It is good practice to have a comment at the start of each section of code and to add comments to explain any tricky bits of logic in the program.

> Visual Basic will convert any comments into green text so it is clear which parts of the code are comments.

Indenting code

Code is also easier to read if it is lined up properly as in this example.

```
Private Sub Command1_Click ()
    If txtInput="Headline text" Then
        txtOutput.Font.Bold=True
        txtOutput.Font.Size=18
        txtOutput.Font.Underline=True
        If txtHeadline="" Then
            MsgBox "Enter text for headline", , "Error"
            txtHeadline.SetFocus
        End If
    End If
End Sub
```

Task 8.6   Calculator

Create a program which will ask the user to enter two numbers. Let the user choose the operator (add, subtract, divide or multiply) from a combo box. Output the answer in a label. A sample is shown in Figure 8.8.

Figure 8.8

Possible improvements:

- check that both numbers have been entered and display an error message
- prevent zero divide errors

- improve the screen display using color, fonts and so on
- reset the values for new calculation
- add an Exit button to stop the program.

Summary

This chapter has looked at:

- making decisions using If . . . Then
- using message boxes
- Select Case
- variables and their use
- data types
- constants.

Starting to function

A *function* is a piece of code built into Visual Basic which carries out a specific operation. The function is called from within your procedure and returns a result to the procedure. Visual Basic has a large number of built-in functions. This chapter looks at some of the more common functions within Visual Basic and how they are used. For more details, Visual Basic Help provides all you need to know.

What are functions?

Using functions saves you work! Operations which would require a great deal of complicated programming can be achieved by a single command. A simple example is the Date function which will give you the current system date. You can use this anywhere in your code to display the date on your form or to set a default date to assist users in using your programs. Other functions help you to display data in the way you want, convert data from one type to another, allow you to work with character data and much more.

The general form of a function is:

```
answer=function name (argument)
```

The argument is a value which is passed to the function. Not all functions have an argument.

Functions can be grouped into various categories:

- mathematical
- string
- date and time
- color
- random numbers
- data conversion

Mathematical functions

Functions are available for finding the square root of a number, performing financial calculations and trigonometry. Some of the functions are shown in Figure 9.1. Use the on-line help for more information.

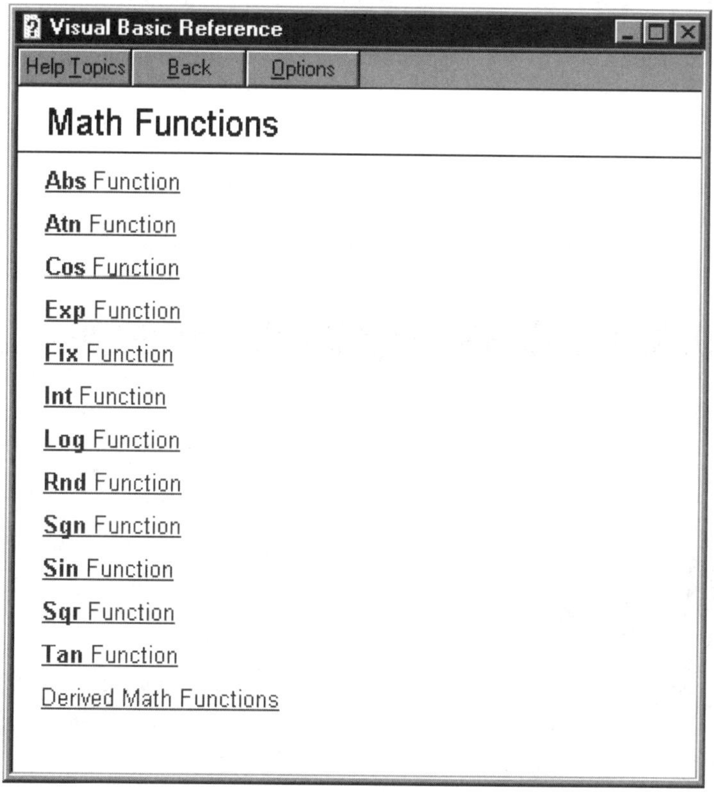

Figure 9.1

Date and Time functions

Function	Returns
Date	date as number
Time	time in 24-hour clock
Now	date and time
Date$	date as character string
Timer	time as the number of seconds since midnight

Start a new project. Create a form with a label in one of the top corners and Blank out the caption.

Write code in the Form Load procedure to set the label caption to the current time.

Add a timer control and set the interval to 1000 (1 second). Add code to the timer event to re-display the time.

Run the program – you should now have a moving time display!

Extensions:

- Experiment with border styles and fonts on the label.
- Add some text boxes to the form – see if the time still counts while you are entering information into the text boxes, as in Figure 9.2.

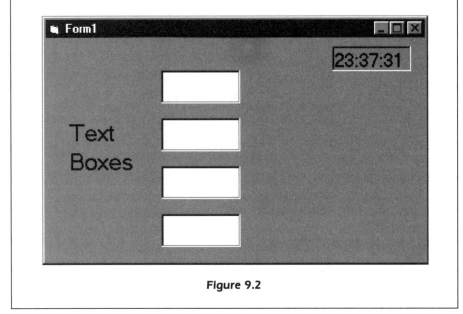

Figure 9.2

Color functions

By now, you have a good grasp of the way that you can use color in your Visual Basic programs. So far, you have set colors of the controls by using properties – BackColor, ForeColor and FillColor as necessary. It is also very useful to change color as the program is running. Visual Basic provides a number of functions which will help you do this.

QBColor function

Returns the Quick Basic color code corresponding to a color number. Quick Basic is a previous version of the BASIC language.

Syntax:

```
colorproperty = QBColor (value)
```

The value argument is a number in the range 0–15. The table shows the QBColor settings:

Number	Color	Number	Color
0	Black	8	Grey
1	Blue	9	Light Blue
2	Green	10	Light Green
3	Cyan	11	Light Cyan
4	Red	12	Light Red
5	Magenta	13	Light Magenta
6	Yellow	14	Light Yellow
7	White	15	Bright White

Task 9.2   Using QBColor

Start a new project. Draw a text box and set the text to blank. Add a set of option buttons labelled with different colors. An example is shown in Figure 9.3.

Write code to change the color of the text box to the color indicated by the option button.

Use the values of QBColor to create the colors.

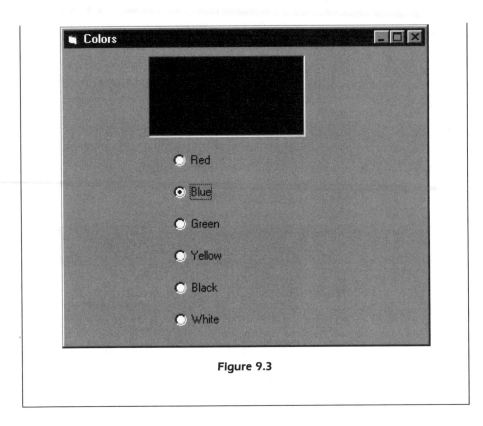

Figure 9.3

RGB function

The RGB function returns a number which represents the RGB color value. The RGB color value gives the relative intensity of red, green, and blue. These produce the color which is displayed.

Syntax:

colorproperty = RGB (red, green, blue)

where red, green and blue are integer values in the range 0–255

RGB (0, 0, 0) is none of any color, and so it gives black
RGB (255, 0, 0) is Red
RGB (255, 255, 255) is maximum intensity of every color, and so gives bright white

If the red, green and blue numbers are the same, it will always give a shade of grey.

Task 9.3   Changing colors using RGB scroll bars

Start a new project. This project is to produce all the possible color combinations from the RGB function. These will be obtained by changing the background color of a text box according to the settings of Red, Green and Blue.

Place a text box, three scroll bars and a Quit button on to the form. Set the Min and Max properties of the scroll bars to 0 and 255 to correspond with the values used in the RGB function. Remember to set Large Change and Small Change.

Add code to the change event of all three scroll bars so that the background color of the text box is set to the RGB value set by the positions of the scroll bars.

Run the program frequently as you work on it. You should be able to change the color of the text box from black (0,0,0) to all the colors available in QBColor (red, green, blue, yellow, and so on), plus many other combinations.

An example of the form is shown in Figure 9.4. Your text box should show white when all scroll bars are at their maximum settings.

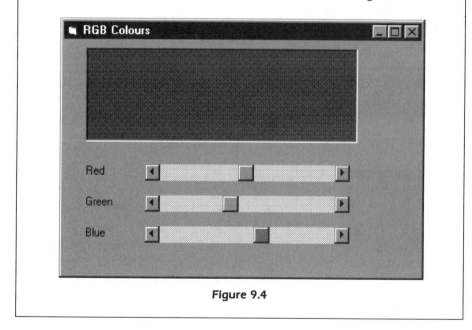

Figure 9.4

Generating random numbers

You will find many occasions when writing programs when it would be useful to have a random value for use within the program- this could be a random line position, color, thickness or shape.

Rnd function

The Rnd function returns a random value between 0 and 1.

Rnd will always produce the same cycle of random values. This is sometimes a problem when you need to have a truly random cycle of values.

Visual Basic has the Randomize statement which seeds the random number generator so it has a different starting point each time. It uses the value of the system timer to set the starting random number.

Random whole numbers

The Rnd function only gives a random number between 0 and 1. If you want a random number between 0 and 15 (for instance when selecting a QBColor), then you have to multiply Rnd by 16.

This may give 8.3467892638. This is because the Rnd function gives a random number to many decimal places.

Int function The Int function gives the integer part of a number without any rounding.

Examples:

Rnd	Rnd * 16	Int (Rnd * 16)
0.2594685	4.151496	4
0.9167534	14.668054	14
0.0094658	0.0567948	0

Task 9.4   Flashing colors

Create a form with a text box and a Stop button. Add a Timer control.
Write code for the Timer control to produce a random number at regular intervals. Use this number in the QBColor function to set the background color of the text box. Experiment with the timer interval to give the best effect.
Run the project frequently as you work on it. You should be able to change the color of the text box to all the colors available from QBColor.
You could also try and make the text box disappear and reappear so improving the flashing of the display.

Don't forget to keep saving your work! You will need it in the next task.

Message boxes and input boxes

Message boxes and input boxes are essentially ways of communicating with the user.

Message boxes

In Chapter 6, you used the message box statement to display messages to the user as the program is running. MsgBox can also be used as a function. The main difference is that the statement displays a message box but cannot do anything with it whereas the MsgBox function can return a value. This value can then be used in the program to make decisions based on the user's choice. You will remember that the message box can have different buttons depending on the value in the type part of the statement.

The function is used in a different way to the statement. As the function returns a value it is assigned to a variable which will then hold the returned value. Brackets must be placed around the expressions in the function.

Syntax:

variable = MsgBox (message[, type] [, title])

You have already seen that the "type" option can specify which icon should be used on the message box. It can also specify which buttons are to be displayed on the message box. This is done by a numeric code as shown in Figure 9.5. If you want both buttons and an icon in the message box you need to add the values together.

MsgBox Function

See Also   Example   Specifics

Constant	Value	Description
vbOKOnly	0	Display **OK** button only.
VbOKCancel	1	Display **OK** and **Cancel** buttons.
VbAbortRetryIgnore	2	Display **Abort**, **Retry**, and **Ignore** buttons.
VbYesNoCancel	3	Display **Yes, No**, and **Cancel** buttons.
VbYesNo	4	Display **Yes** and **No** buttons.
VbRetryCancel	5	Display **Retry** and **Cancel** buttons.
VbCritical	16	Display **Critical Message** icon.
VbQuestion	32	Display **Warning Query** icon.
VbExclamation	48	Display **Warning Message** icon.
VbInformation	64	Display **Information Message** icon.
VbDefaultButton1	0	First button is default.

Figure 9.5

For example, a message box like that in Figure 9.6 which says "Are you sure?" with a question mark (32) and Yes and No buttons (4) would have a type value of 36 (32 + 4):

answer = MsgBox ("Are you sure?", 36)

Visual Basic returns a value to indicate which button the user has clicked. In the example given, this is stored in the variable **answer**.

Button	Value returned
OK	1
Cancel	2
Abort	3
Retry	4
Ignore	5
Yes	6
No	7

Task 9.5   Are you sure?

Open your last project.

Change the code on the Quit button to display a message box saying "Are you sure" with Yes and No buttons. Add an icon if you like.

An example is shown in Figure 9.6.

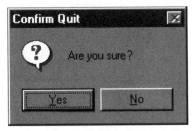

Figure 9.6

Write code to make the program exit only if the Yes button is clicked.

Input box

Input box displays a dialog box on the screen ready for the user to input some data and then waits for the user to click on OK. The OK and Cancel buttons are part of the input box and do not require any coding from you.

The syntax of the function is:

InputBox (prompt[, title][, default])

The input box shown in Figure 9.7 has a prompt of "Please enter your name" and a title of "Input Box".

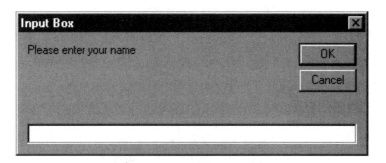

Figure 9.7

The code line for this is:

x = InputBox("Please enter your name", "Input Box")

The value typed into the input box will be in the variable **x** if the user clicks the OK button. This can then be used in the program. If the Cancel button is clicked the function returns an empty string.

Different versions of Visual Basic have input boxes which look slightly different. Do not worry – they all work in the same way.

The default part of the command syntax allows you to specify a value to be used as a default value. This could be used when dates are to be entered – the input box could default to today's date as the most frequent value, as in Figure 9.8.

If the prompt is quite long, the text will be wrapped on to another line. You can control where this happens by inserting a carriage return character (Chr(13)) and a linefeed character (Chr(10)) between each line. Chr is covered in the next section.

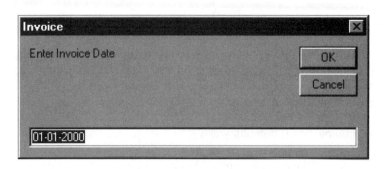

Figure 9.8

Chr function

Every character on the keyboard has an associated value. This is known as the ASCII value. The ASCII values can be found in the Visual Basic help if you are interested. You do not need to worry too much about this but there are some useful values which are associated with special codes.

The Chr function returns the character defined by the ASCII value. The values you are likely to need while programming are:

Code	Character
8	backspace
9	tab
10	linefeed
13	enter
65	A
66	B
	etc.

Using Chr   The command

x = InputBox("Please type the name of the person" & Chr(13) & "who is selling this property", "Property Sale")

produces the input box shown in Figure 9.9.

& is an operator which joins character strings together.

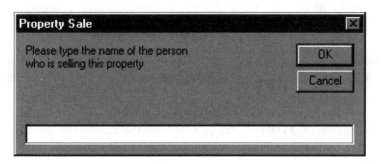

Figure 9.9

Task 9.6   Making a list

Start a new project. Put a list box and a command button named Add on to the form.

Write code for the Add button to display an input box prompting the user for a new item to add to the list box. Only add this text to the list box if the user clicked on OK; do nothing if the user clicks on Cancel.

Changing data type

Visual Basic has several functions which convert between different data types. The Conversion Keyword Summary Help screen gives a list of the conversion functions. This section concentrates on the commonly used conversion functions.

Str

Str converts numeric data to character string.

x = Str(number)

Str leaves a space at the front of the string to contain the sign of the number. If negative, the first character is a minus sign, if positive the first character is blank.

Format function

The Format function formats a number, date, time, or string according to the format specified in a format expression.

X = Format (value, "format string")

value is the numeric or string data to be formatted
format string is a string of characters which specify how the data is displayed

Examples:

Function	Returns
x = Format (Date, "dd/mmm/yy")	gives the date in the form 28/Mar/97
x = Format (Date, "dddd dd mmmm yyyy")	gives the date in the form Friday 28 March 1997
x = Format (number, "##,##0.00")	displays a number with leading zeros suppressed, a comma separator and 2 decimal places

Format can also be used to convert numeric data to character string. To do this, leave out the format string. The command becomes:

x = Format (number)

The resulting string does not have the leading space that you get when using the Str function.

Val

The Val function is used to convert character strings to numeric values. It will convert all numbers and is able to recognize decimal points. Blanks and other symbols will be ignored. Strings containing other characters will return a value of zero.

X = Val (string)

x = Val ("123.4")	gives 123.4
x = Val ("Hello")	gives 0
x = Val ("1 2 3")	gives 123

Manipulating strings

Visual Basic has a number of functions which help you work with character strings.

Function	Description
LCase (string)	converts string to lower case
UCase (string)	converts to upper case
Len (string)	gives length of string
Trim (string)	removes spaces at the start and end of strings
Left (string,n)	extracts n characters from the left of the string
Right (string,n)	extracts n characters from the right of the string
Mid (string, x, n)	extracts n characters from the middle of the string starting at the position x. If n is omitted Mid extracts all characters from position x to the end of the string.
Instr (string1, string2)	compares string2 with string1 and returns the position of the start of string2 within string1

Examples:

Take the string " Hello World "

Note that the string has a space at the start and end.

Function	Returns
LCase (string)	" hello world "
UCase (string)	" HELLO WORLD "
Len (string)	13
Trim (string)	"Hello World"
Left (string,5)	" Hell"
Right (string,5)	"orld "
Mid (string,3,2)	"el"
Instr(string, "ell")	3

Check the Visual Basic help for more details of these and many other functions.

Task 9.7   Name please! ───────────────────────

Start a new project.

Create a form similar to that shown in Figure 9.10. The Full name box is a text box; Surname and First Name should both be label controls.

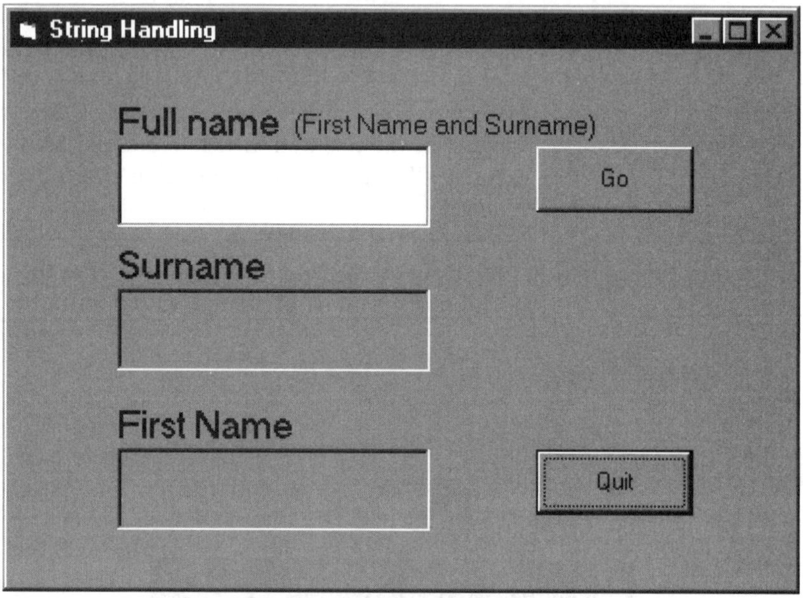

Figure 9.10

Make the Go! button search for the space in the full name. If no space is found, produce a message box saying it cannot find a space. Otherwise, take the portion to the left of the space and print it in First Name. Take the portion to the right of the first space (use Mid) and put this into the Surname box.

Test your application. What happens if somebody enters three names?

Summary

This chapter has looked at some of the many functions available in Visual Basic:

- date and time
- color
- random numbers
- message box
- input box
- changing data type
- manipulating strings
- formatting.

Drawing with controls

Visual Basic is a Windows language offering a full range of graphics capabilities. There are two ways of using graphics in Visual Basic. Graphics controls are covered in this chapter and allow lines, shapes and images to be placed on a form. The other way of using graphics is with graphics methods, which are covered in Chapter 13.

Graphics controls are used for drawings placed directly on to a form to add color and interest. Visual Basic has several graphics controls. These are used in a similar way to the previous controls, except that they rarely have code attached to them.

There are five graphics controls in Visual Basic:

Control	Use
Line	drawing lines
Shape	drawing rectangles, squares, ovals and circles
Image	displaying graphics files
Picture Box	providing an area for drawing with graphics methods
Frame	grouping together other controls

Line control

Line controls are used whenever you want to draw lines on a form. This could be to separate different areas on a form. Lines can have different widths, colors and styles.

To place a line control on the form:

- Select the line control icon (shown above) from the toolbox.
- Click on the form where the line is to start.
- Drag with the mouse to the end point of the line and release the mouse button.

Figure 10.1 shows the properties of the Line control.

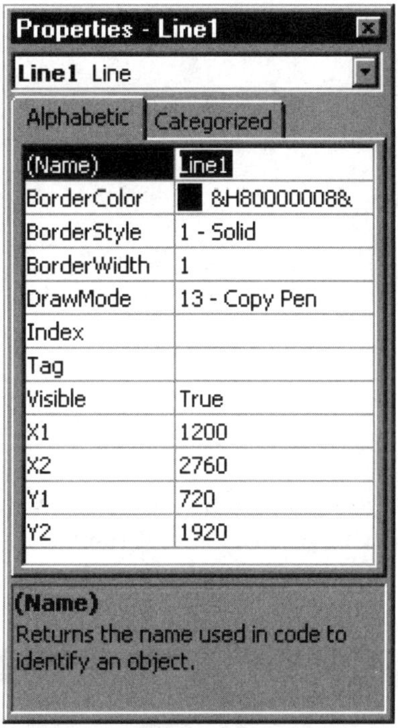

Properties - Line1	☒
Line1 Line	▼

Alphabetic	Categorized

(Name)	Line1
BorderColor	■ &H80000008&
BorderStyle	1 - Solid
BorderWidth	1
DrawMode	13 - Copy Pen
Index	
Tag	
Visible	True
X1	1200
X2	2760
Y1	720
Y2	1920

(Name)
Returns the name used in code to
identify an object.

Figure 10.1

Changing the position of the line

You may recall that the position of most controls is given by Top, Left, Height and Width properties. The line control is different from these because it uses an X1, X2, Y1 and Y2 set of properties, as shown in Figure 10.2.

X1 is the distance from the LEFT of the form to the START of the line
Y1 is the distance from the TOP of the form to the START of the line
X2 is the distance from the LEFT of the form to the END of the line
Y2 is the distance from the TOP of the form to the END of the line

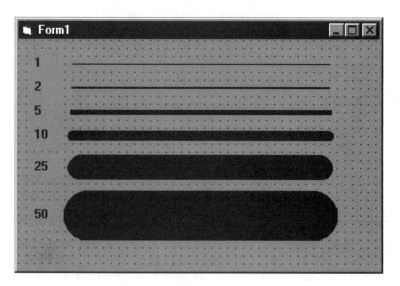

Figure 10.2

Changing the thickness of the line

The thickness of the line is controlled by the BorderWidth property. Any values are acceptable, although 1 to 10 give the best results.

Some different line thicknesses are shown in Figure 10.3.

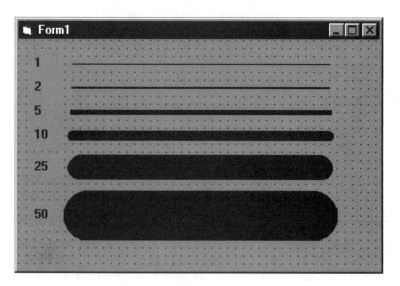

Figure 10.3

Color

The BorderColor property allows you to select the color of the line. This is done by double clicking on the property and selecting from the palette.

Style

The BorderStyle property allows you to create different styles of line, solid and dotted. It can be set at design time using the menu in Figure 10.4, or can be changed at run-time by changing the BorderStyle property.

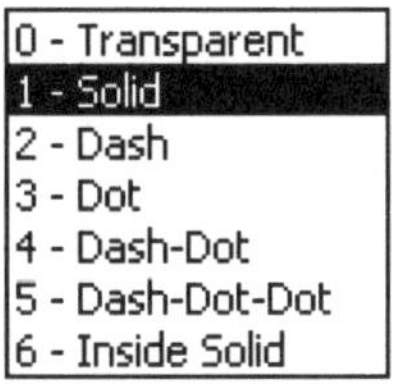
0 - Transparent
1 - Solid
2 - Dash
3 - Dot
4 - Dash-Dot
5 - Dash-Dot-Dot
6 - Inside Solid

Figure 10.4

Task 10.1 Lines!

Create a form which contains a line control, a check box and a set of option buttons to control the style and thickness of the line.

A sample form is shown in Figure 10.5.

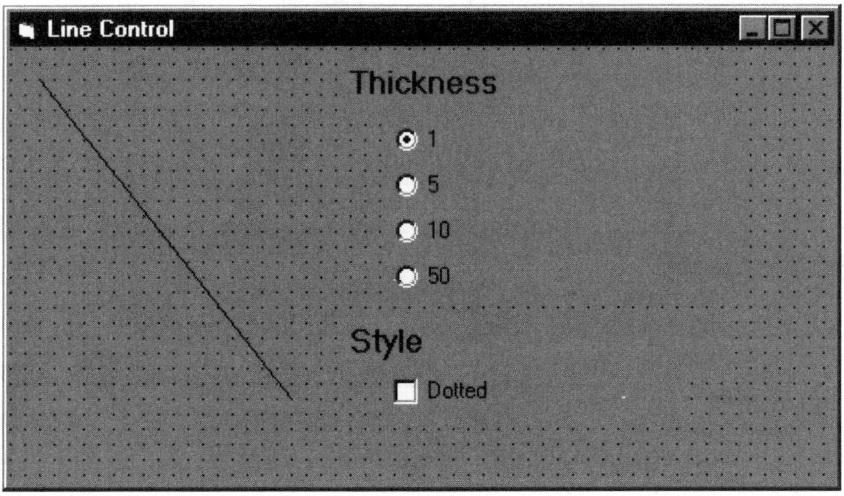
Line Control
Thickness
1
5
10
50
Style
Dotted

Figure 10.5

Add code to change the thickness and style as appropriate.

Shape control

Drawing shapes in Visual Basic is different from most other Windows packages. Visual Basic has one control to draw rectangles, squares, ovals and circles. Most packages (such as Paint) have different tools for each shape.

Shapes are drawn in the normal way. All shapes start as a rectangle and are then changed by setting the Shape property.

Changing the shape

The Shape property of the Shape control allows different shapes to be created, as shown in Figures 10.6 and 10.7.

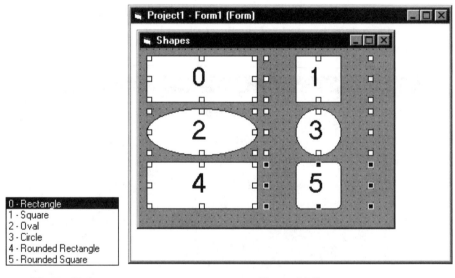

| 0 - Rectangle |
| 1 - Square |
| 2 - Oval |
| 3 - Circle |
| 4 - Rounded Rectangle |
| 5 - Rounded Square |

Figure 10.6   **Figure 10.7**

The white (or blue) handles show the corners of the shape control. For the rectangles and oval, these are at the corners of the control. For the squares and circle, the shape does not take up all of the available space in the control.

Changing colors and patterns

The color of a solid shape is changed by the BackColor property. The BackStyle property can either be Opaque or Transparent. BackStyle is Transparent by default, and so must be changed to opaque for your chosen BackColor to appear.

Different patterns are available to fill the shape. FillStyle sets the pattern for the shape. The options are shown in Figure 10.8.

```
0 - Solid
1 - Transparent
2 - Horizontal Line
3 - Vertical Line
4 - Upward Diagonal
5 - Downward Diagonal
6 - Cross
7 - Diagonal Cross
```

Figure 10.8

The table below summarizes the properties you should set for different types of fill.

Fill	Example	BackStyle	BackColor	FillStyle	FillColor
Unfilled		Transparent	N/A	Transparent	N/A
Filled		Opaque	The color required for the shape	Transparent	N/A
Patterned with the form as a background		Transparent	N/A	The pattern required	The color of the pattern
Patterned with a colored background		Opaque	The color of the background	The pattern required	The color of the pattern

The colors of the shape can be controlled with the BackColor, BorderColor and FillColor properties. These change the colors of different parts of the shape. The diagram in Figure 10.9 shows a shape filled with a pattern with the different properties labelled.

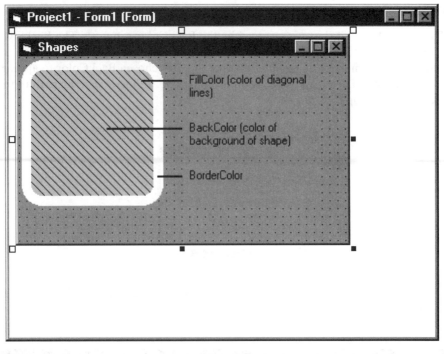

Figure 10.9

Task 10.2   UFO

Draw a UFO using shape controls (and also line controls). This will be used in the task at the end of the chapter. An example is shown in Figure 10.10.

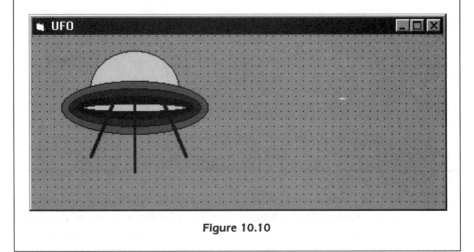

Figure 10.10

Pictures in Visual Basic

As well as simple shapes, Visual Basic can display pictures on your forms. Pictures are used to add visual interest to a form. The pictures are pre-created graphics files, which can be drawn in a paint package and saved, loaded from clip-art libraries, or scanned from pictures or photographs.

The image control

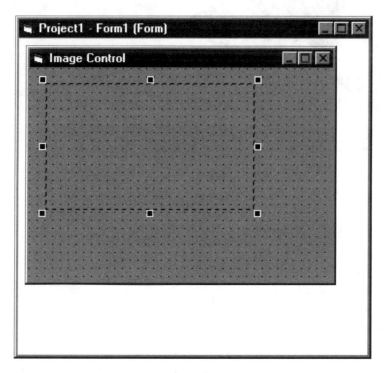

The image control is used to display graphics files. The types it will display are bitmap files (usually .BMP from Paint), icons (usually .ICO from an icon library) and metafiles (.WMF). Version 5 can also display GIF and JPEG files (from the Internet).

Image controls are placed on a form in the normal way.

Figure 10.11

The image control will initially appear as a dotted rectangle, as in Figure 10.11. This rectangle will not appear when the program is running.

Displaying graphics files

The Picture property specifies the file name of the picture to display. Picture will initially say (None). When ▓ is clicked (or the property name is double-clicked), a standard open dialog box appears.

Some pictures come supplied with Visual Basic. You may have installed these with Visual Basic, otherwise they may be loaded directly from the CD version. A library of icons is also supplied with Visual Basic, and an image control will display these as well. You can, of course, use scanned images or create and save your own pictures in Paint ready for use in Visual Basic.

The form in Figure 10.12 has an image control showing a BMP file.

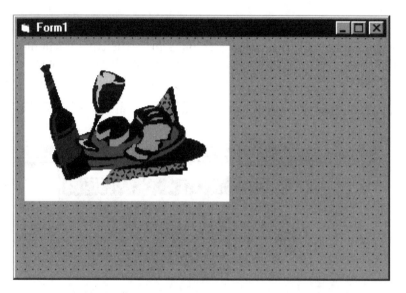

Figure 10.12

Appearance and border styles

- The Appearance property selects a Flat or 3D image.
- The BorderStyle property draws a border around the image.

Sizing an image

If the blue handles at the corners are dragged to a different shape and a bitmap is being used, the image will be normally be cropped so only the top-left portion of the image is visible. With the Stretch property set to True, all the picture will be visible and so the size of the picture will change. With Stretch set to False, the image will be cropped so only the top-left portion is visible. This is shown in Figure 10.13.

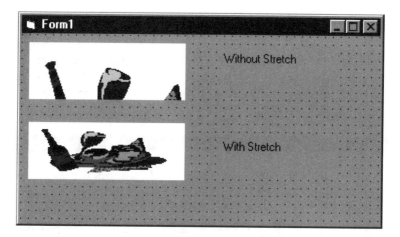

Figure 10.13

If a metafile (.WMF) is used, then the image will be resized to fit the new space whether or not the Stretch property is set to true.

Picture box control

A picture box control has three uses:

- displaying graphics files
- containing other controls
- acting as a canvas for graphics methods (this is explained in Chapter 13).

Displaying Graphics Files

A picture box can display graphics files. The picture is loaded in the same way as for an image control.

An image control is normally better than a picture box because it gives greater flexibility about how the image is displayed. A picture box also requires more memory than an image control.

The Picture Box is normally only used to display graphics files when graphics methods are used to draw on top of the picture (see Chapter 13).

Containing other controls

A picture box can act as a container for other controls. This means that when new controls are placed in the picture box, their top and left co-ordinates are measured relative to the picture box instead of the form. Also, if the picture box is moved, all the controls inside the picture box move with it, as shown in Figure 10.14.

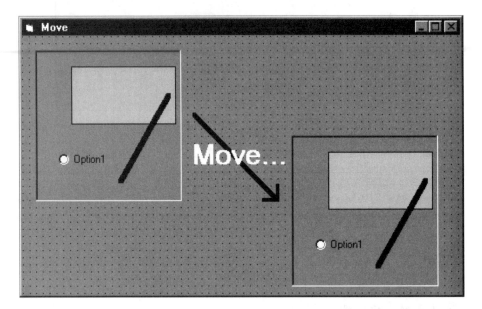

Figure 10.14

This can be very useful for grouping graphics controls together to form a shape.

The border can be turned off by setting the BorderStyle property to None. This makes the picture box invisible to the user, while still containing the other visible controls. If the Visible property of the picture box is set to False, then all the other controls inside the picture box will also disappear.

Frame control

The frame control acts as a container (similar to a picture box) by grouping together other controls and giving them a collective heading. A good use of a frame control is to group a set of option buttons. Using frames, you can have more than one set of option buttons on the same form.

The frame control is drawn on the form in the usual way. An example frame is shown in Figure 10.15.

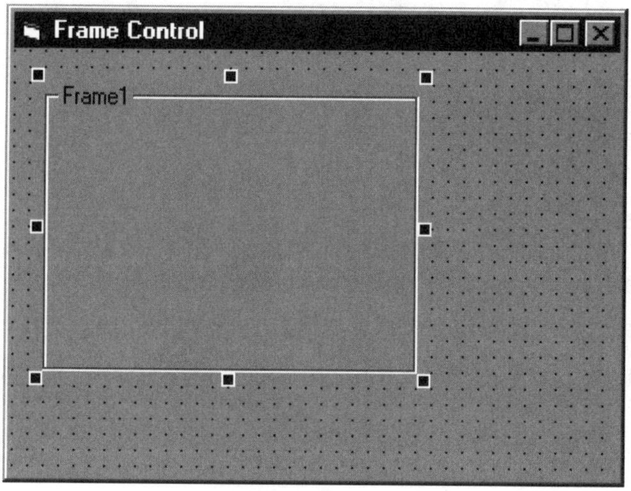

Figure 10.15

Other controls can now be placed inside the frame. This means that they can be moved as a group: move the frame and any objects inside the frame also move. Controls inside the frame belong to the frame and cannot be moved out of it. To remove a control from a frame you have to use **Cut**.

The differences between a frame and a picture box for use as a container are:

- a frame allows a title to be given to the container
- a frame requires less memory than a picture box
- a picture box can have its border hidden.

___ **Task 10.3   Move me!** _____

Create a frame on a form and put four image controls inside it. Make the four image controls display arrows for up, down, left and right (these can be found in the icons).

Add code to the images so that when they are clicked, the frame, including the arrows, moves in the direction of the arrow by a set amount.

A sample screen is shown in Figure 10.16.

An improvement could be to stop the frame from going off the screen.

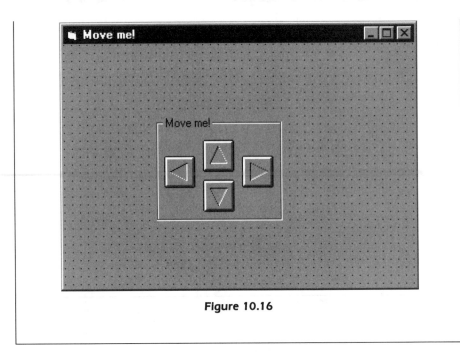

Figure 10.16

Using the UFO drawn out of shapes in the shape control section earlier in this chapter, it can be animated so it will fly across the screen.

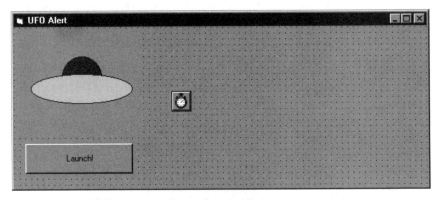

Figure 10.17

If you have not already drawn a UFO, draw one now using shape controls.

Insert a picture box control. This will act as a container for the UFO shapes. Remove the border from the picture box. Put the UFO shapes inside the picture box.

This cannot be done by moving the shapes because they just get placed on top of the picture box, instead of inside it. To get them inside the picture box, they must be selected, then cut to the clipboard. The picture box should then be selected, and the UFO shapes pasted back in. Check this has worked by moving the picture box. The shapes should move as well.

Add a timer control to the form. Set the interval to about 100. Ensure the enabled property is set to False. Add code to the timer event so that the ship is moved 100 units to the right.

Add a command button and label it Launch. Make the command button enable the timer when clicked. A sample form is shown in Figure 10.17.

Run the program!

Possible enhancements:

- Add a reset button to stop the UFO and return it to the start position.
- Make the UFO come back for a return journey after it reaches the right-hand edge of the screen.

Summary

In this chapter you have:

- drawn using line controls
- learnt about different shape controls
- used the frame control
- grouped controls together
- animated basic shapes.

⎔ 11 ⎔ Going round in circles

One of the reasons computers have been so successful is that they can keep going without getting tired for much longer than people can. And they can keep on getting the answers right! It is very easy to write a program with a few lines of code which will take several hours to run. Or you can make it run for ever if you like. This chapter extends your knowledge of the programming language with a look at some new code structures.

Looping in Visual Basic

Looping is very important in programming. Many programs require an operation or a series of operations to be repeated many times. All programming languages provide at least one way of coding a group of repeating commands. Visual Basic has two different types of repetition commands, the For . . . Next loop and the Do . . . Loop command. The For . . . Next loop is used when the commands are to be repeated a specific number of times, whereas the Do . . . Loop command repeats until a condition is satisfied. However, it is usually possible to use either of the commands and you can choose which is best for each program.

For . . . Next loops

The For . . . Next command repeats a group of commands a specified number of times. The syntax of the command is:

```
For counter = start To end [Step increment]
    statement block
Next counter
```

The For command must come first – this is what tells Visual Basic that a For . . . Next loop follows. Counter is a numeric variable which is used to keep count of the number of times the loop has been executed. Start and End specify the starting and ending values of the counter.

There can be any number of lines between the For and the Next command. These can include any Visual Basic commands. The commands within the loop are executed in turn.

The final line is the Next command. When the program reaches this point it increases the value of the counter. The counter is normally incremented by 1 but can be incremented by any other amount, for example 2, 10 or -1 by specifying this as a Step parameter on the For command.

The value of the counter is then checked against the end value of the For loop. If the new value of the counter is greater than the end value, the loop finishes and the program continues with the line of code after the Next statement. If it isn't, the statements in the loop are executed again.

An example could look like this:

```
For i = 1 to 10
    lstName.Additem i
Next i
```

This For . . . Next loop adds the value of i to a list box. At the end of the loop, the list box will contain the numbers 1 to 10.

Nested loops

You can have a number of loops inside each other. These are known as *nested* loops. You will need to give each loop a different variable name as its counter.

Example:

```
For i = 1 To 3
    For j = 1 To 3
        answer = i * j
    Next j
Next i
```

This example will perform the calculation i * j nine times (3 * 3). The order of the calculations is shown below:

i	j	Answer
1	1	1
1	2	2
1	3	3
2	1	2
2	2	4
2	3	6
3	1	3
3	2	6
3	3	9

Interrupting loops

While Visual Basic is inside a loop, all the computer's processing power is used to perform the calculations in the loop. It has no time left to update the screen display or get input from the user.

Refresh

You can force it to update the screen by using the Refresh method.

Object.Refresh

For example:

lblName.Refresh

would update the contents of the label.

DoEvents

DoEvents forces the computer to check for input from the user. This makes it possible to respond to mouse clicks or key presses while in a loop. To use it, type the command

DoEvents

inside the loop.

> You will no doubt create loops which you cannot get out of! These are often due to errors in your program! You can use Ctrl-Break to get out of a loop so you can correct the code or add the DoEvents command if appropriate.

__ **Task 11.1   Loop the loop**_____

- Create the form shown in Figure 11.1.
- Name the text box txtCalc.
- Attach the following code to the Go command button.

```
For i = 1 To 10
    For j = 1 To 10
        For k = 1 To 10
            txtCalc.Text = i * j * k
        Next k
    Next j
Next i
```

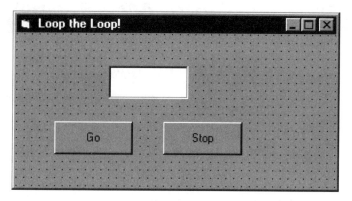

Figure 11.1

- Make the Stop button end the program.
- Run the program. Click on Go.

You will find that it runs but all that happens is that there is a short pause then the number 1000 appears in the text box.

To make it run properly you need to change the code to refresh the display after each calculation. You will also need to slow the program down – you can do this by coding another For . . . Next loop which contains no other statements. Remember to use a different variable as the counter. You will need to experiment with the End value to find a suitable value to give a speed which shows the values as they change.

You should now discover another problem! – you can't interrupt the program. Use Ctrl-Break to interrupt the program and add a DoEvents statement inside the k loop. You should now be able to stop and start the program.

If you wish to explore this further you could try making the Stop button store the current values of the counters and make the Start button restart from the same place.

You can also create a loop in Visual Basic using the Do . . . Loop statement. This has two variations – you can repeat a block of statements *while* a condition is true or *until* a condition becomes true. The variation used depends on whether the condition is placed on the Do statement or on the Loop statement and on whether the While form or the Until form is used.

Do	Loop

Do [{While | Until} *condition*]
 	
    [*statementblock*]
 	
Loop
	Do
	
	    [*statementblock*]
	
	Loop [{While | Until} *condition*]

The Do command must come first – this is what tells Visual Basic that a Do Loop follows. A Do While executes while the condition remains true. A Do Until executes until the condition becomes true. The condition is a numeric or character expression. The condition is coded in the same way as conditions for If . . . Then commands which are in Chapter 8.

There can be any number of lines between the Do and the Loop command. These can include any Visual Basic commands. The commands are executed in turn.

The final line is the Loop command. If the condition is no longer true, the loop finishes and the program continues with the next line of code after the Loop statement. If it is still true the statements in the loop execute again.

The example used in the previous section can also be written as a Do . . . Loop – using any of its variations. The code would look something like this:

Do While	Loop While	For

i = 1
Do While i <= 10
   list1.Additem i
   i = i + 1
Loop
	i = 1
	Do
	   list1.Additem i
	   i = i + 1
	Loop While i <= 10
		For i = 1 to 10
		   lstName.Additem i
		Next i

Do Until	**Loop Until**	

i = 1
Do Until i > 10
   list1.Additem i
   i = i + 1
Loop
	i = 1
	Do
	   list1.Additem i
	   i = i + 1
	Loop Until i > 10	

As for the For . . . Next loop used in the last section, this loop adds the value of i to the list box. At the end of the loop, the list box will contain the numbers 1 to 10.

Compare the two examples – using a Do . . . Loop you have to set the starting value of the counter and increment the counter yourself. For . . . Next loops are better for this example because they automatically increment the value of i.

As for For . . . Next loops, you can have a number of Do . . . Loops inside each other.

The previous example would look something like this:

```
i = 1
j = 1
Do While i <= 10
    Do While j <= 10
        answer = i * j
        j = j + 1
    Loop
    i = i + 1
Loop
```

For this calculation, using Do . . . Loops is much more complicated than using For . . . Next loops.

Task 11.2 Number cruncher 1

Create a program to calculate and display the square of every number from 0 to 10,000. Create a list box to display the numbers. Make it long! Add command buttons for Go and Stop. Add a Close button.

Write code to calculate each square and add to the list box.

The Stop button is to stop the calculation. Pressing Go should restart from the beginning.

Don't forget the DoEvents command can be very useful.

You might like to try making the calculation start again from the point at which it was stopped.

Task 11.3 Number cruncher 2

Modify the program so the list box shows both squares and roots for each number.

Chr(9) will insert a tab in a list box.

Summary

In this chapter you have:

- used For . . . Next loops
- used Do . . . Loop
- learnt how to break into loops.

12 Making it work

It's rare for any program to work first time, especially long and complicated programs. Finding the errors in the programs can be difficult and time-consuming. Visual Basic, in common with most programming languages, provides a range of facilities to assist you in finding and correcting errors.

Errors in programs are often referred to as "bugs", and hence, removing the bugs from a program is called debugging!

There are three main sorts of error:

- syntax errors which are errors in writing the code. These are caused by mistyping or getting the syntax wrong and are fairly easy to pick up.
- run time errors which cause the program to fail when it is run
- logic errors which occur when the program appears to run correctly but does the wrong thing! These are a lot more difficult to find.

Syntax checking

Every command and function in Visual Basic has a specific syntax (a way in which it must be entered). If the syntax is slightly wrong, the program will not work. Errors in syntax may be mistyped function names, missing brackets or too few parameters.

Visual Basic helps you find these errors. You will undoubtedly have already noticed it when typing in code. A window appears saying that there is a mistake in the line you have just typed.

For example, the following code (in the Form Load) procedure is clearly incorrect:

```
Form1.BackColor = QBColor(5
```

When you press Enter, Visual Basic will automatically detect the mistake, and display a message box as in Figure 12.1.

> The offending line will appear in red.

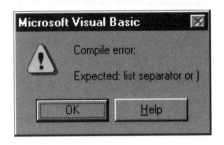

Figure 12.1

This is very useful, it means that many mistakes you make while programming will be picked up even before the program is run. This is different from most traditional programming languages which only find errors when the program was compiled or run.

Compile checking

Visual Basic performs a *compile check* when you run a project. This picks up errors in your code which are not syntax errors. For example, it would pick up an If statement without an End If or a For without a Next statement. This is quite a frequent mistake, particularly when you have nested loops or Ifs. This is easier to do if you make sure that code is indented so you can see where the Ifs and loops start and end.

Task 12.1   Bugs 1

Add the following code to a Form Load procedure:

```
For color = 0 to 15
    Form1.BackColor = QBColor(color)
    Form1.Refresh
```

Do not put a Next on the end. Now run the project. You will see an error box as in Figure 12.2.
    The mismatch will be picked up and the error indicated.

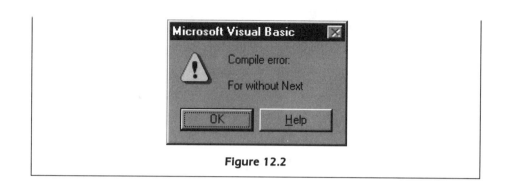

Figure 12.2

Run-time errors

As well as all the errors which Visual Basic picks up before you run the program there are other errors which are only picked up when the program is running.

Sometimes you may mistype an object name or forget you changed its name. When you use the name in the code Visual Basic will accept it. However, when the line containing the error is processed the computer will pick it up. A similar error occurs when you try to use a variable name which has not been declared or set.

Task 12.2 Bugs 2

Add the following code to the Click event of a command button on a new form. Presume you have mistyped Form as From, as below:

```
From1.BackColor = QBColor(5)
```

The line will be accepted when you press Enter because its syntax is correct. Now run the project, and click on the command button. You should see a dialog box as in Figure 12.3.

Microsoft Visual Basic

Run-time error '424':

Object required

| Continue | End | Debug | Help |

Figure 12.3

The End button will stop the project and return you to the code. The debug button will pause the project, and highlight the line which contains the error. It is usually then easy to pick up the error.

Stopped and paused projects

A project can be in three different states: running, stopped and break mode.

- Stopped is the normal mode where you can design the forms and code the application.
- When a project is running, although the code can be viewed, it cannot be changed.
- When in break mode, execution is suspended; the forms remain as though they were running, except they cannot be used. In break mode, the debugging tools can be used and the code can be edited.

You can break into a program either by clicking Debug when a run-time error occurs, or by clicking on ▌▌ from the toolbar, or by pressing Ctrl-Break. Ctrl-Break is especially useful if your project is locked in a loop which makes the mouse inoperative.

Break mode is very useful because it lets you interrogate the state of variables at the point of execution using the debugging tools. Data tips will give you the current value of the variable as the mouse is moved over the variable name. When in break mode, the project can either be continued from the point where the break was activated, or the project can be re-started, or the project can be stopped completely.

Debugging while running

A wide range of facilities is available to help you track down errors while the program is running. They are available from the **View** menu. In Visual Basic version 5 they are also available from the Debug toolbar, shown in Figure 12.4.

Figure 12.4

Locals window

Visual Basic version 5 also has a *Locals* window. This shows all the variables which currently have values when the program is stopped. The programs you have created so far do not use many variables, but for more complicated applications with more variables it is very useful. An example is shown in Figure 12.5.

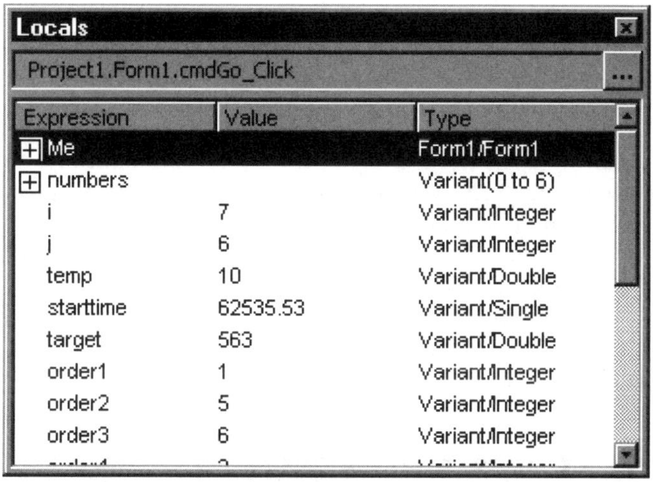

Locals		
Project1.Form1.cmdGo_Click		...
Expression	Value	Type
⊞ Me		Form1/Form1
⊞ numbers		Variant(0 to 6)
i	7	Variant/Integer
j	6	Variant/Integer
temp	10	Variant/Double
starttime	62535.53	Variant/Single
target	563	Variant/Double
order1	1	Variant/Integer
order2	5	Variant/Integer
order3	6	Variant/Integer

Figure 12.5

Immediate window (Debug window in versions 3 and 4)

The immediate window lets you interrogate the current state of variables and properties in the program. Because it is active in a break in the program, the variables will be filled with "live" data from the program. The most useful way of interrogating is by using the Print command. This will display the value of the variable tested on the next line of the immediate window.

You can also interact with the form in other ways. As well as interrogating properties, you can also set properties and do anything which you can using code. You enter the commands in the window in the same way as you would in a code window. The difference is that they are executed immediately on pressing Enter.

Try creating a form with a command button on it. Break into the program and set the caption of the command button by typing in the Immediate window:

Command1.Caption = "New caption"

You can also display and change properties:

Print Command1.Top
Command1.Top = Command1.Top + 100

Breakpoints

Breakpoints can be put into a section of code to automatically break into the program at that point. This can be useful if you are having problems with a particular section of code and wish to break into it at a set point to check the variables. A breakpoint works in the same way as pressing Ctrl and Break when that line is being executed.

To add a breakpoint, put the cursor on the required line. Select **Toggle Breakpoint** from the **Run** menu, or click the 🖑 button on the Debug toolbar. This will highlight the appropriate line in red as shown in Figure 12.6.

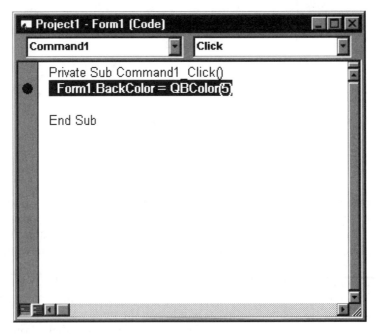

Figure 12.6

Now when the program is run it will switch into break mode when it reaches this line. Now you can test the variables in the Locals and Immediate windows. Afterwards continue the program again as normal.

You can have as many breakpoints as you require. To switch off a breakpoint, select the line and choose **Toggle Breakpoint** again. Or choose **Clear All Breakpoints** from the **Tools** menu.

Stepping through programs

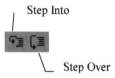

Step Into

Step Over

If you want to examine your program more carefully the **Step Into** and **Step Over** options let you work through your program a line at a time. This has the same effect as having every line as a breakpoint. After a line of code has been processed you can test the variables to find out what has happened. Then use the Step Into or Step Over command to execute the next line.

Step Into and Step Over are the same, except for what they do when they reach a procedure. Step Into will work through a procedure line by line, whereas Step Over would execute the procedure all at once. There is more about procedures in Chapter 17.

Avoiding errors

The debug facilities will help find those elusive bugs. However, there is no substitute for programming it correctly in the beginning. You should take preventative steps when coding the program to make it easier to find any bugs which do occur:

- Always name controls descriptively so you can remember what they do
- Indent your code so that it is easy to spot mismatched commands
- Add comments to your code so that when you look back at it you can remember what it does.

You will find this makes bug finding much easier!

Summary

In this chapter you have:

- looked at different types of error
- used the Debug toolbar
- used the Local, Immediate or Debug windows
- learnt about breakpoints
- stepped-through a program.

13 Drawing without controls

Visual Basic has two ways of drawing graphics. You have already used one method when you used graphic controls in Chapter 10. The second drawing method is to use graphics methods from within your programs to draw in a container control.

The methods are quite different. Graphics controls are created at design time. They can be changed and moved by making changes to the properties from within the code, but it is very difficult to create new graphics controls while the program is running. Graphics methods make it much easier to draw graphics features at run-time. This makes it possible to produce moving and changing displays.

When you draw using graphics methods the lines and shapes do not become controls. Instead, they form part of a picture held in the container control. This can make it tricky to move shapes made of several parts using the graphics methods. Often the best solution is to use some graphics controls and some graphics methods: the best of both worlds!

Container controls

A container control is required to use graphics methods. The container control provides the "canvas" where the picture is drawn. Only two types of control can be used as a container for graphics methods: the form and the picture box.

The form is sometimes used if the whole screen is required as the drawing area, for instance in the screen saver at the end of the chapter. More usually the drawing is confined to a particular area of the form – in which case a picture box control is used.

Scales and co-ordinates

A picture box has scale properties, as shown in Figure 13.1.

The standard unit of measurement is the twip. A twip is used because it is a measurement which is independent both of screen dimensions and printer resolution. You have already seen that the twip is used in Visual Basic for measurements such as heights and positions of controls.

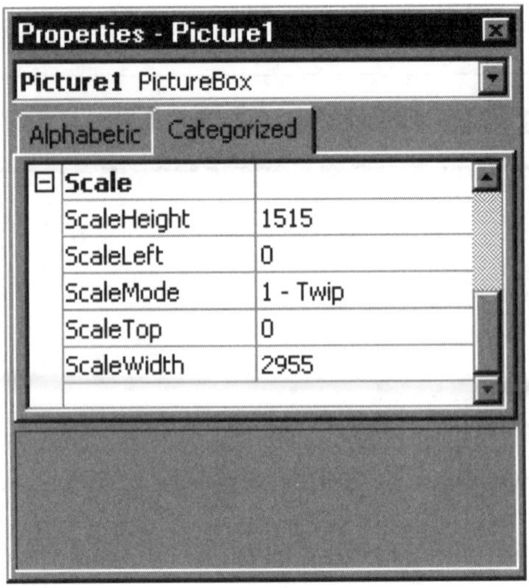

Figure 13.1

The ScaleHeight and ScaleWidth properties are the vertical and horizontal dimensions of the drawing area. The ScaleHeight property is slightly less than the Height property (and ScaleWidth is slightly less than Width). This is because the scale properties are the size of the inside of the drawing area, whereas the Height and Width properties are the size of the control. The difference is the border width.

Each point in the picture box is referred to by two co-ordinates. The first specifies the distance of the point from the left-hand edge of the picture box (x co-ordinate). The second co-ordinate gives the distance of the point from the top of the box (y co-ordinate). Therefore the top left is 0, 0 and the bottom right is ScaleHeight, ScaleWidth. Any point within the container can be referred to in this way.

Figure 13.2 shows some example co-ordinates in a picture box.

All graphics methods (lines, circles, rectangles, etc.) use this co-ordinate system for specifying points.

Drawing dots

A dot is the simplest shape that can be drawn. To draw a dot on the form, use the following command:

object.Pset (x, y)

object is the name of the container control in which the dot is required (usually a picture box)
x is the distance from the left of the picture box (in twips)
y is the distance from the top of the picture box (in twips)

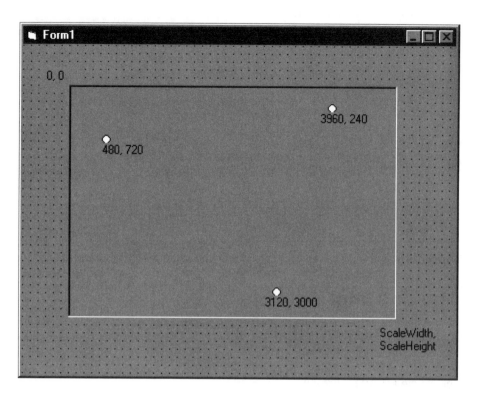

Figure 13.2

Changing styles

Size The size of the dot is controlled by the DrawWidth property. This operates differently from the DrawWidth property of the Line control. If you change the DrawWidth property of the Line control after it is created, the thickness changes. With graphics methods, the DrawWidth (and ForeColor, FillColor, FillStyle, BorderStyle and many more) properties of the picture box only affect new shapes drawn in the picture box. The old shapes remain unaffected.

Color You can change the color of the dot by setting the ForeColor property of the picture box. Use the QBColor function to select the color.

```
pctName.ForeColor = QBColor(4)
pctName.Pset (100, 100)
```

This would draw a red dot on the form. The same effect can be replicated by:

```
Picture1.Pset (100, 100), QBColor(4)
```

The option after the last comma is an optional extra which allows the color of the dot to be specified.

object.Pset (x, y), color

Drawing lines

You can draw a line between two points in a picture box by using the Line method. The syntax is as follows:

object.Line (x1, y1) – (x2,y2)

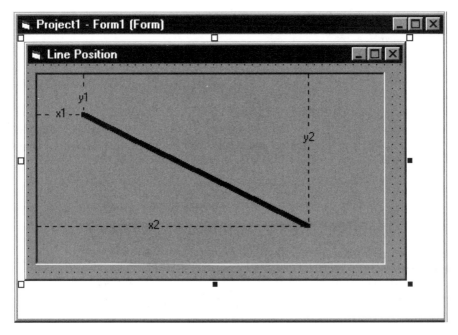

Figure 13.3

object is the name of container control in which the line should be drawn
x1 is the distance from the left edge of the picture box to the start of the line
y1 is the distance from the top of the picture box to the start of the line
x2 is the distance from the left edge of the picture box to the end of the line
y2 is the distance from the top of the picture box to the end of the line

This is shown in Figure 13.3.

For example, to draw a line from the top left of the screen to a point 1000 twips from the left and 500 twips from the top you would write:

pctName.Line (0, 0) – (1000, 500)

Task 13.2   Line by line

Start a new project. Draw a large picture box taking up most of the form, and add a command button labelled Random Line.

Add code to the button so that when it is clicked, a line is drawn from a random start point to a random end point within the picture box.

> A random number between 0 and 1 is given by RND (check out Chapter 9). To get a random number between 0 and the width of the picture box, use RND * pctBox.ScaleWidth.

Save the project – it will be used for further tasks.

Changing styles

The default line is a thin black line. It is possible to change the color of the line and also the thickness and style of the line.

Color   You can change the color of the line in two ways. The first is to change the ForeColor property of the picture box. This is a way of changing the default color for all lines. If, however, you just want to draw one line in a different color, then this can be added on to the end of the Line command. The color is referred to by using the QBColor function (see Chapter 9).

object.Line (x1, y1) – (x2,y2), color

Example:

pctName.Line (100, 500) – (1000,600), QBColor(4)

Width The thickness of a line can be specified by the DrawWidth property of the picture box control. The DrawWidth must be set before the line is drawn, changing it afterwards will have no effect on any previously drawn lines.

Line style You can change the style of the line by using the DrawStyle property of the picture box. Again, it must be set before the line is drawn.

Drawing rectangles

Rectangles (and squares) are just an extension of the Line command. The co-ordinates work in the same way, so x1, y1 gives the top left-hand corner and x2, y2 gives the bottom right-hand corner. Check Figure 13.3 to remind you of the co-ordinates. The B at the end of the command specifies a box instead of a line.

object.Line (x1, y1) – (x2,y2), color, B

This will draw an un-filled rectangle. If the default color is to be used, the color parameter can be left out, but the comma must remain:

object.Line (x1, y1) – (x2,y2), , B

To draw a filled box, the last option should be BF.

object.Line (x1, y1) – (x2,y2), color, BF

This will fill the shape with the currently set ForeColor. The FillStyle and FillColor are ignored for rectangles drawn with BF. If you want to draw a rectangle filled with a different color or patterned, the FillStyle and FillColor properties must be set and then the B option used.

Task 13.3   Shaping up

Change your random line project so that when the user clicks on the button it chooses a random shape (line, rectangle or filled rectangle). Also include random colors and random thicknesses.

Automate the process by using a Timer control to draw the shapes instead of a command button.

Drawing circles

The Circle method is used. The syntax is as follows:

object.Circle (x, y), radius [, color]

object is the name of the container control
x, y are the co-ordinates of the centre of the circle
radius is the distance in twips from the centre to the edge of the circle

The color of the inside of the circle is set by the FillStyle and FillColor properties of the picture box. To get a solid colored fill, set FillStyle to 0 – Solid and the required FillColor.

___ Task 13.4   More shapes _____

Extend the random shapes project to include circles. Include random fills for the shapes. An example is shown in Figure 13.4.

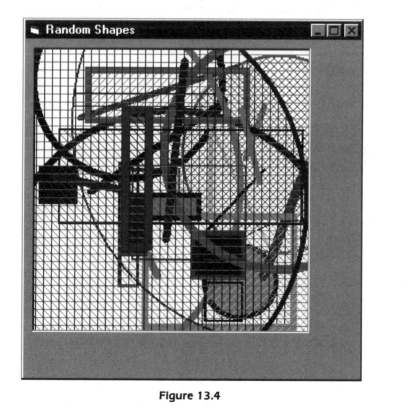

Figure 13.4

Print method

In most older versions of BASIC and other programming languages the Print command would be one of the first things learnt. In Visual Basic, the main way of displaying information on the screen is by the Label controls. However, Print still exists, and can be used for adding text to a picture box. Used in this way Print is a graphical method which draws text.

The syntax is:

object.Print "Text to be printed"

The location of the text is specified by the CurrentX and CurrentY properties.

> CurrentX and CurrentY specify the location of the next drawing method. They are usually set to the last place an object was drawn. For example, if you have plotted a point at (100, 200), then CurrentX would be 100 and CurrentY would be 200.

The following example would print Hello at (200,300).

```
pctName.CurrentX = 200
pctName.CurrentY = 300
pctName.Print "Hello"
```

Changing styles

ForeColor specifies the color of the text. You can change the font and size of the text using the Font property of the picture box in a similar way to a label. Note that the font property has to be changed before the text is printed.

Example:

```
pctName.CurrentX = 200
pctName.CurrentY = 300
pctName.Font.Name = "Times New Roman"
pctName.Font.Size = 24
pctName.Print "Hello"
```

AutoRedraw

The AutoRedraw property applies to the picture box and form objects. It specifies whether or not any drawing produced using graphic methods should be re-drawn when another window obscures the view.

An example of this can be shown by using a variation on the screen saver produced above. If another window is moved on top of Figure 13.4 and then removed, the screen will look like Figure 13.5.

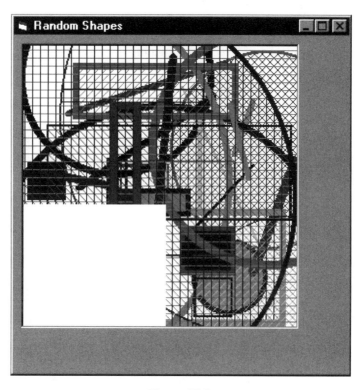

Figure 13.5

The part where it has been overlaid with another window does not get redrawn, but instead returns to the background color. This can be overcome by setting the AutoRedraw property to True. This will redraw any parts which become hidden.

Task 13.5   Random shapes screen saver!

Throughout this chapter you have been creating a Random shapes screen saver. Some final touches are now required:

- Set the Caption of the title bar to nothing. Set MaxButton, MinButton and ControlBox to False. This ensures that the form has no title bar.
- Set the WindowStyle of the form to 2 so that it is maximized automatically.
- Add code to the Form Activate event so the picture box resizes to fill the whole space available. The code to do this is shown in Figure 13.6.

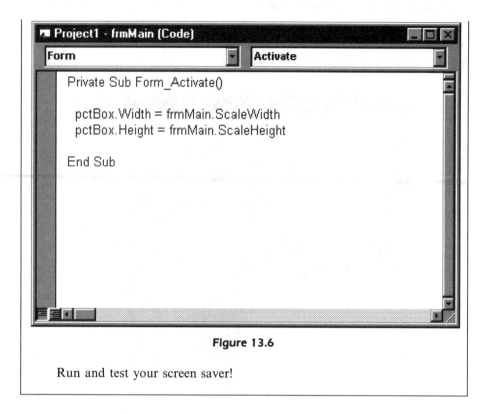

Figure 13.6

Run and test your screen saver!

Summary

In this chapter you have:

- used a picture box as a container
- drawn lines, rectangles and circles using graphical methods
- displayed text using Print.

Adding menus

All Windows applications use menus. Look at the top of the Visual Basic screen and you will see a set of Windows menus. Visual Basic contains a menu editor which makes it easy to create your own menus for your applications. You can easily add menus to your applications created in Visual Basic.

Creating menus

There are two steps to creating menus for your application:

- design and create the menu layout
- add code to the menus

You can add menus at the start of producing your application, or at the end, or you can add menu options as you work. This is the usual approach: as you add more features to your application, you will add options to the menus.

The Menu Editor

You can access the Menu Editor either by choosing **Menu Editor** from the **Tools** menu, or by clicking on the ▣ button from the toolbar. This will display a window as in Figure 14.1.

Each item on a menu has to have a Caption (the text displayed) and a Name. As for all names in Visual Basic, menu options should have a standard prefix. This could be something like menu or m_.

To add a new item to a set of menus:

- Type the text to be displayed in the Caption section
- Enter a Name for the menu item
- Click on Next or press Enter.

Figure 14.2 shows a File menu being added.

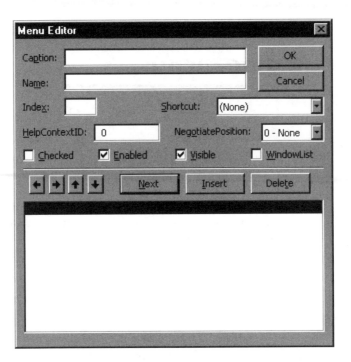

Figure 14.1

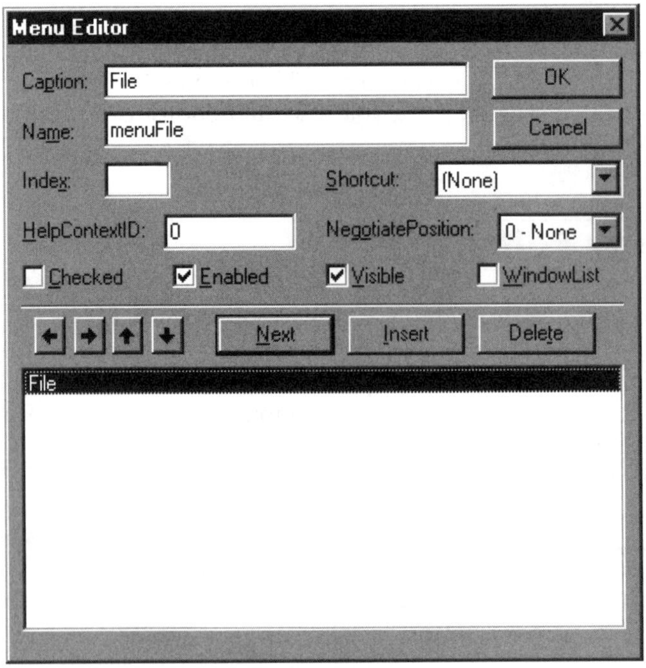

Figure 14.2

Start a new project. Open the Menu Editor. Create two menu items in the list. Then close down the Menu Editor and look at the form. It should look like Figure 14.3.

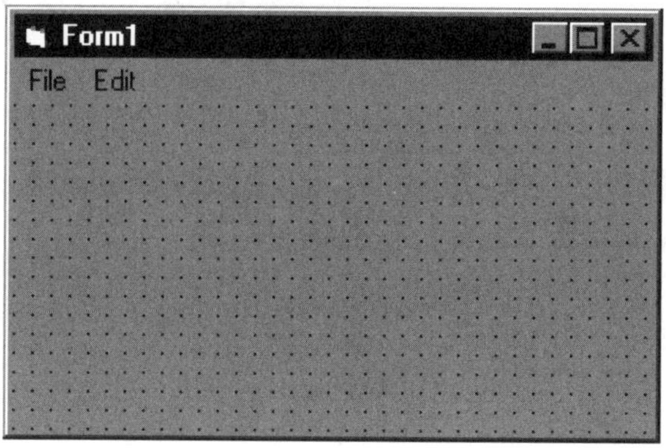

Figure 14.3

Both menus appear on the menu bar which is automatically created. Try clicking on one of the menus. You will notice that a menu is not pulled down, but instead a code window is displayed. This is because no options have yet been added to the menu titles.

Adding options to menus

Menus have a title and a number of options which appear when the title is clicked. In the Menu Editor window the menu title is at the left of the box and options on the menu are listed underneath the title indented by a set of dots.

The ➡ button indents a menu option. Figure 14.4 shows an example of a menu system.

Notice that the options which appear on the File menu (New, Open, Save and Exit) are indented and listed underneath the File heading. The Options menu contains a Color submenu (containing Red, Blue and Yellow). These options are double indented so they appear on a submenu. The menus created by this structure are shown in Figure 14.5.

The Red, Blue and Yellow options are on a submenu of the Color option.

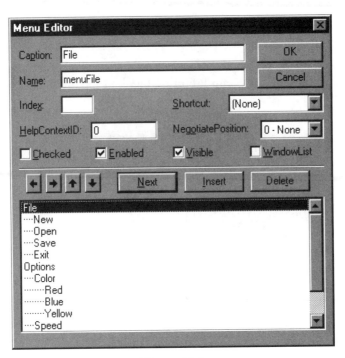

Figure 14.4

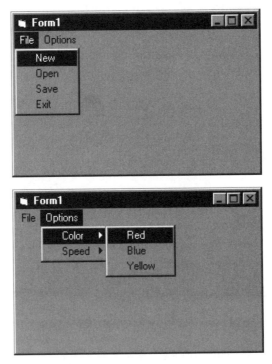

Figure 14.5

Separating menu options

If you look at most Windows menus, you will see separation lines, as shown on the menu in Figure 14.6.

Figure 14.6

Separators make it easy to group options on a menu together. You can create separators in Visual Basic.

To insert a separator, set the caption of a menu option to a single hyphen (-). Even though a separator cannot be clicked upon it still needs to be given a name. An example is shown in Figure 14.7.

Keyboard control

Alt and underlined letter

Alt and an underlined letter from the menu name is the usual way of using the keyboard to access menus. Visual Basic allows you to select which letter should be underlined giving you greater control over your application.

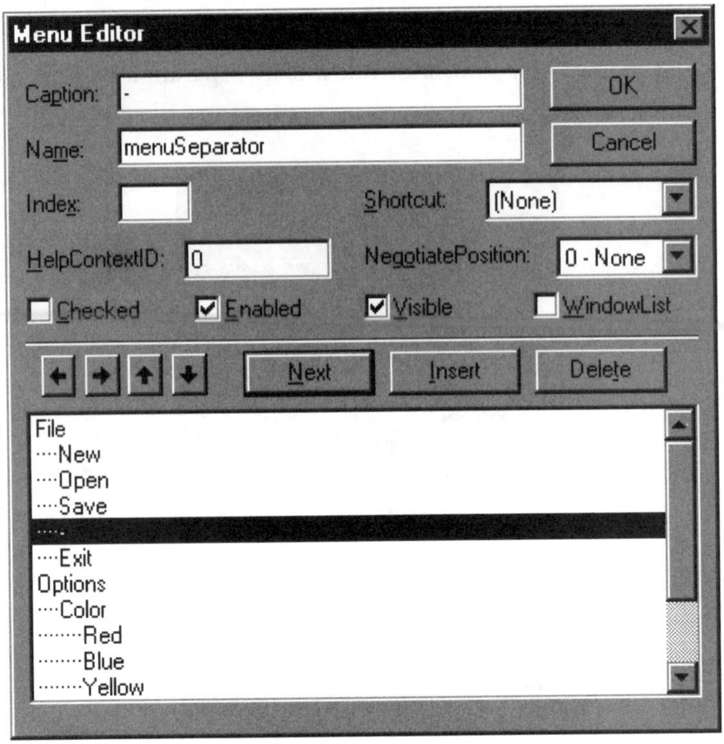

Figure 14.7

To define an underlined shortcut key, insert an ampersand (&) in front of the shortcut letter. The caption in the Menu Editor box will display as an &. When the dialog box is closed this will appear as an underline.

For example:

- &File will display File
- O&ptions will display Options.

This same technique can also be used for options on the menus as well as the menu titles themselves. A sample menu using shortcuts is shown in Figure 14.8.

It is usual to have the first letter as the shortcut letter, unless that particular letter has already been used for a different menu. However, there is one exception. The x in Exit is always underlined in Windows applications.

Shortcut keys

A shortcut key is a quick way of selecting a option from a menu without actually opening the menu. For example, Ctrl and V may be used for Paste and F2 for New Game.

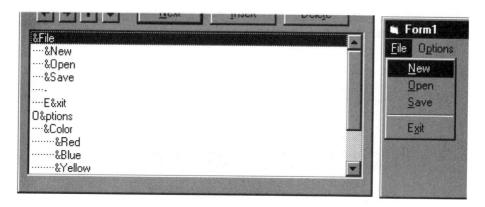

Figure 14.8

Shortcut keys can be assigned to a menu option from the Shortcut combo box in the Menu Editor, as shown in Figure 14.9.

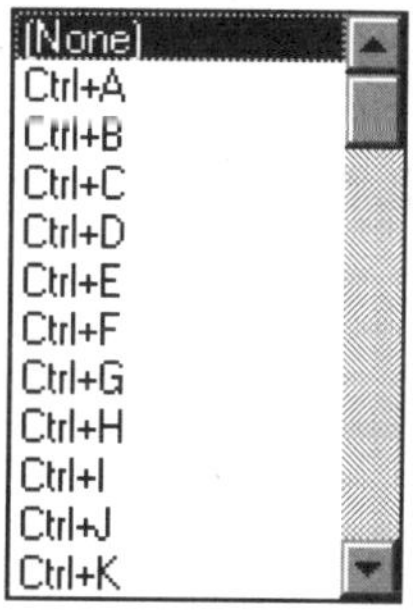

Figure 14.9

You can assign Ctrl and any key, the function keys, and combinations of Shift, Ctrl and different keys. Notice that when you set a shortcut key, this appears next to the option on the menu, as in Figure 14.10.

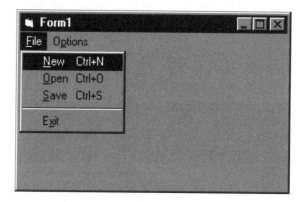

Figure 14.10

Adding code to menus

Code can only be added to a menu option once it has been created. Each menu option acts like a control – it is listed in the Objects section of the Code window as shown in Figure 14.11. The only event available for a menu is the Click event.

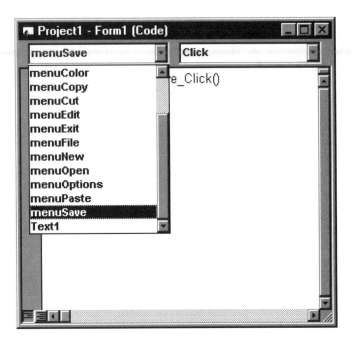

Figure 14.11

Code is added to a menu option in the same way as for a command button. Often, you may wish to use the same code for a menu option and an on-screen command button. The best way to do this is to make both the menu option and command button call the same subroutine. Details of how this is done are in Chapter 17.

You can also view the code window for a menu option by clicking on the menu option from the design view. This opens up the correct code event and has a similar effect to double-clicking on a control.

Task 14.2 Changing properties of a shape using menus

Set up a form which contains a shape control.

Add sets of menus to control the shape, size and color of the shape. An example is shown in Figure 14.12.

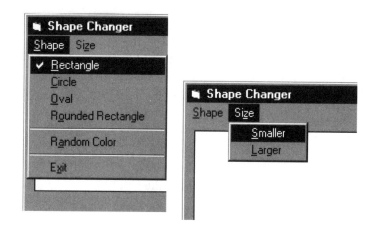

Figure 14.12

Add code to the Shape menu options to set the Shape property. Make the Random Color option change the color of the shape to a random QBColor value. Set up Ctrl and C as a shortcut to change color. Add a check to ensure that the new color selected is not the same as the previous color.

Add code to the Exit option to leave the application.

On the size menu make the Smaller option reduce the height and width of the shape by a set amount (100 works well). Code the Larger option in a similar way. Add a check to ensure that the height and width never drop below zero or exceed the dimensions of the form. Add shortcut keys to Smaller and Larger, perhaps F5 and F6.

Save, run and test your project.

Advanced features

Activating and deactivating menus

You can make menus invisible in the same way as controls, by setting their Visible property. You can either remove a whole menu or just an option from the menu.

It is also possible to "grey out" options from a menu when they are not available. This is used extensively in Windows applications; you can see a good example by looking at the **View** menu in Visual Basic itself. Menus or menu options are greyed out by using their Enable property.

Using checked menu options

Menu options can also be used in a similar way to check boxes and option buttons. You can set the Checked property so a small tick ☑ appears next to the option. This could be used to indicate that Bold text is switched on or to select a color from a list. If you are using ticks to ensure that only one option in a group can be selected, the other options in the group must be switched off. This does not happen automatically as for a set of option buttons.

For example:

```
menuRed.Checked = True
menuBlue.Checked = False
menuYellow.Checked = False
```

switches on the Red option and switches the Blue and Yellow options off.

Control arrays

You can create control arrays of menu options. This can be useful when you have many options performing a similar task. To create a control array, set the Name to a common value and enter the Index number in the Index box. A good example is choosing a starting level from 1 to 10 in a computer game. Control Arrays are explained in Chapter 15.

Summary

In this chapter you have:

- added menus to your application
- added code to these menus
- used shortcut keys
- learnt how to enable and disable menu options.

⬡ 15   **Arrays**

An array can be thought of as a filing system for controls and variables. An array is a set or group of related items. Each item in an array is accessed by an index number which represents its position in the group. In Visual Basic there are two types of array: control arrays and variable arrays.

Control arrays

A control array is a set of controls on a form, all of which have the same name. Because they have the same name, they all call the same code procedure.

Control arrays are used where you want many of the same type of control, all of which will serve a similar function. This may be a set of option buttons or a set of similar images.

Each item in a control array is distinguished from the others by the Index property. This a numerical value which starts at 0 for the first control and increases for each subsequent control in the array. The Index property is very important when adding the code for the controls because it tells you which item in the control array has been clicked.

Creating a control array

The simplest way is to:

- draw a control, and set its name property to the name for the control array
- copy that control to the clipboard
- paste it in again (see Chapter 5).

You will see a box as shown in Figure 15.1.

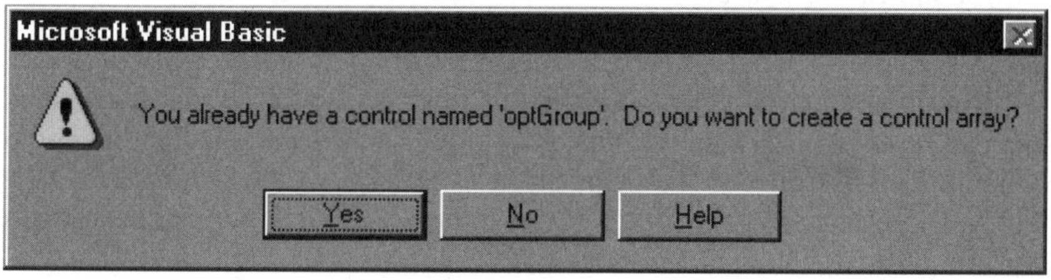

Figure 15.1

If you choose No, a control will be created with a new name. If you choose Yes, a new control is placed on to the form with the same name as the original. Look at the Index property and you will notice the new control has an Index of 1. The original control now has an Index of 0.

Task 15.1   Control arrays

Create a set of option buttons, all with the same name, for selecting font sizes. They should be labelled: 8, 12, 18, 24, 30, 36.

Place a text box on the form. Enter some text in the Text property. The option buttons will change the size of the text. An example is shown in Figure 15.2.

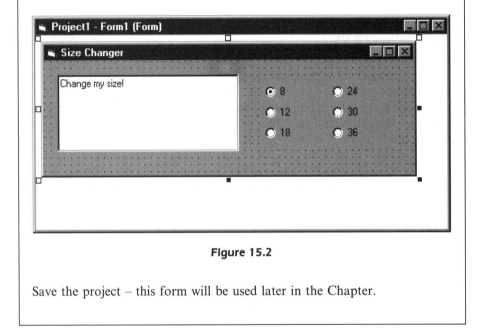

Figure 15.2

Save the project – this form will be used later in the Chapter.

Adding code to control arrays

Look at the Click procedure for the option buttons, as shown in Figure 15.3.

You will see that the Private Sub line is different from most Click procedures. It includes an extra parameter, **Index as Integer**. **Index** is a variable that contains a value indicating which of the items in the control array was clicked. **As Integer** specifies the data type of the index. For instance, if the first control in the control array was clicked, this has an Index value of zero, and the value of the Index variable in this procedure would then also be zero.

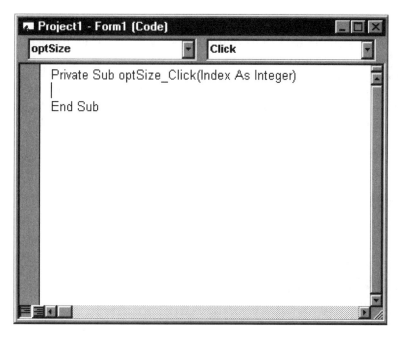

Private Sub optSize_Click(Index As Integer)
|
End Sub

Figure 15.3

 Task 15.2   Control arrays 2

Using this method, you can add code to the Click event of the option
button control array to change the size of the text box to the appropriate
value.

> This is a good place to use a Select Case because there are six options all
> of which are changing the same property.

 Run and test your program.

Another use of the control array is when you have a set of image controls
which form a grid. This can be used to display pictures, and is useful in finding
out which image has been clicked. This is used in games involving graphic shapes
such as Noughts and Crosses or Kim. An example of using it is shown by the
Noughts and Crosses program in Chapter 19.

Changing properties of items in a control array

As you have seen, an item in a control array is referred to by the name of the control array followed by the Index number of the item in brackets. The items in the control array have the properties of the control. For example, each item in an image control array has the properties of an image box. This means that properties can be changed within your code in the normal way. You can write code to change a property of a single control in the array, multiple controls or the complete control array.

For example, to change the background color of an image box with index number 5, you would write:

```
imgArray(5).BackColor = QBColor(4)
```

Variable arrays

A variable array is a set of variables which are related in some way such as months of the year, or a set of sales figures. The data stored in the array must all be of the same type. The array stores the variables with a single name. Like control arrays, each item in the array is referred to by an index number showing the position in the array.

Usually an array is dimensioned in the declarations part of the code. This makes it accessible to all the procedures associated with the form. It is possible to set up an array inside a procedure but this is rarely done.

The Dim statement is used to tell Visual Basic about the array and allocate the storage space. The Dim statement is similar to that used for variables but specifies the number of items in the array:

```
Dim Name(Size) as Type
```

Name is the name of the array
Size is the number of items in the array
Type is the type of variable which is stored in the array (see Chapter 8).

> The array actually contains one more item than the value given by size. This is because there is an index value 0 as well.

Once declared, an array is used in a similar way to normal variables except it has multiple entries. Individual items in the array can be accessed using the name of the array, followed by the index number of the item you wish to access.

Example: the following code sets up and fills a ten item array with random numbers between 0 and 99:

In the declarations section:

```
Dim ArrayRand(10) As Integer
```

In the form load procedure:

```
For i = 1 to 10
    ArrayRand(i) = Int(Rnd * 100)
Next
```

Multiple dimension arrays

Variable arrays can have more than one dimension. One-dimensional can be likened to all the items being laid out in a list. A two-dimensional array is more like a grid, as shown in Figure 15.4.

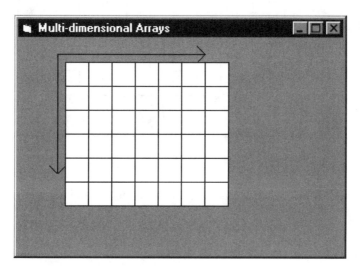

Figure 15.4

Each item has two numbers to locate it: the distance along the top and the number of squares down. It is like a co-ordinate system or a spreadsheet.

A two-dimensional array is defined as below:

```
Dim ArrayName(a, b) As Type
```

where a and b are the sizes of each dimension of the array. For example, if a was 3 and b was 5, there would be 15 squares where values could be stored.

```
ArrayName(3, 4) = 10
```

This would set the value of the item 3 along and 4 down the array to 10.

More dimensions are possible, but it is rare to use more than a two-dimensional array. The more dimensions used, the harder it becomes to visualise. For example, three dimensions is like having a cube, as in Figure 15.5, where each smaller cube holds information. Four dimensions or more becomes a nightmare!

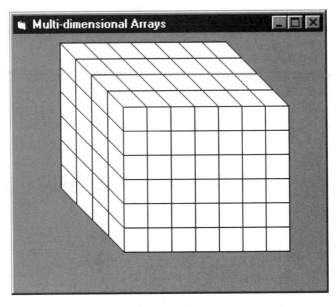

Figure 15.5

A two-dimensional array is used in the Noughts and Crosses program in Chapter 19.

Task 15.3   Lottery number selector

Set up a form with six labels in a control array named lblNumbers. Add a button marked Select, as in Figure 15.6.

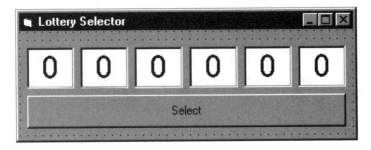

Figure 15.6

In the declarations sections, set up an integer array to hold six numbers. Call it LotteryNumbers.

When you click on the Select button, six random numbers between 1 and 49 should be picked. This requires a loop. At the moment, just select a random number for each of the six numbers, and store the number in the LotteryNumbers array. The number then needs to be displayed as the caption of the appropriate label.

Run and test the program.

After a few goes, you will notice that it sometimes picks the same number more than once. This can never happen in the lottery, and so your program needs to check for this. If the number the computer selects has already been selected for a previous ball, then it must pick another number. This is not required for the first ball, as there are no previous balls to check it against. For subsequent balls, the test is necessary. This will require a second loop to check the balls inside the first loop.

Some more to try:

• Make it automatically select when the form is loaded
• Make the labels into ball shapes
• Include the possibility of selecting more than one set of numbers (requires two dimensional arrays).

Summary

In this Chapter you have:

• created control arrays
• added code to control arrays
• used variable arrays
• learnt about multiple-dimension arrays.

Using more than one form

Visual Basic projects can contain more than one form. This adds flexibility by allowing separate forms for particular purposes; this might be for data entry or to display graphic screens such as a *splash screen* which displays when the application starts. If you start to write applications of any size, multiple forms become essential.

Adding additional forms

The button on the toolbar will add another form to your project. If you are using Visual Basic version 5, then you will see an Add Form options box, as in Figure 16.1.

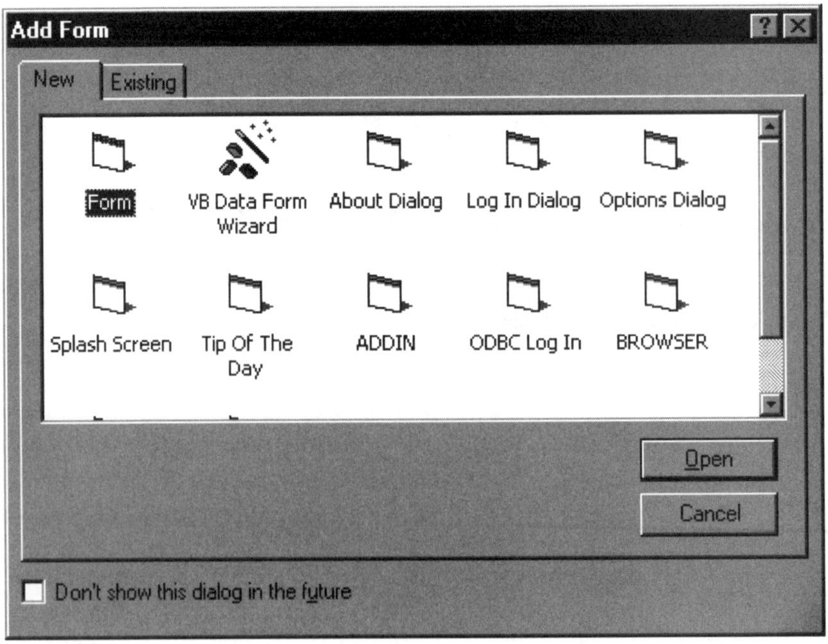

Figure 16.1

The Form option at the top left will give you a blank form, and this is the most usual option. The Data Form wizard is used if you are creating database applications, and it will automatically set up an input form for you. All the other form options are pre-made forms which you can add to your application. They are not complete, but give you a good starting point for a new form.

Users of versions other than Visual Basic 5 will not see this dialog box and will immediately be presented with a blank form.

Additional forms can have controls and code attached to them in exactly the same way as for the original form. By default the second form will be called Form2. As for a control it is advisable to change the name of the form to something more memorable, for example frmInput. When you have only one form in an application the name is not so important as you do not use it as a reference. When you have more than one form in your application the name of the form is used to make up a unique reference for any control within the project.

For example, a text box used for input of a name would be referred to as:

frmInput.txtname

Switching between forms

The Project window can be displayed either by clicking on from the toolbar, or by choosing **Project** from the **View** menu. This will show you the Project window, as in Figure 16.2. This now shows that the project has two forms. You can easily switch between the forms by selecting the required form from the list and then choosing the Code or Form button.

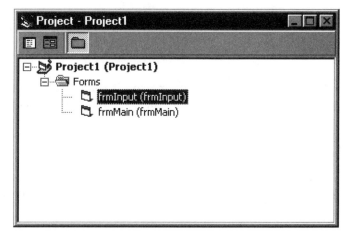

Figure 16.2

Displaying forms

Additional forms are not very useful if they cannot be displayed! Each form has three possible states, as follows:

State	Description
Not loaded	This is the normal state for additional forms.
Loaded but not displayed	In this state, the form has been loaded so its controls and variables are accessible, but it is not displayed on the screen.
Displayed	The form is loaded so its controls are accessible, and it is active on the screen so it can receive user input.

The following commands change the state of the form:

Command	Action
frmName.Show	If the form is not loaded, this loads and displays the form. If the form is already loaded, this displays the form.
Load frmName	This loads the form but does not display it.
Unload frmName	This removes the form from the memory and removes it from the screen.
frmName.Hide	This removes the form from the screen, but keeps it loaded.

A form can also be loaded without an explicit command. If you refer to a control on an unloaded form from within the code, the form will be loaded.

Task 16.1   Launcher

Start a new project. Add three command buttons to the form. Label them Show, Hide and Exit as shown in Figure 16.3. Add a second form to the project. Display a picture (any will do) on this form.

Add code to the Show and Hide buttons to display and remove the second form.

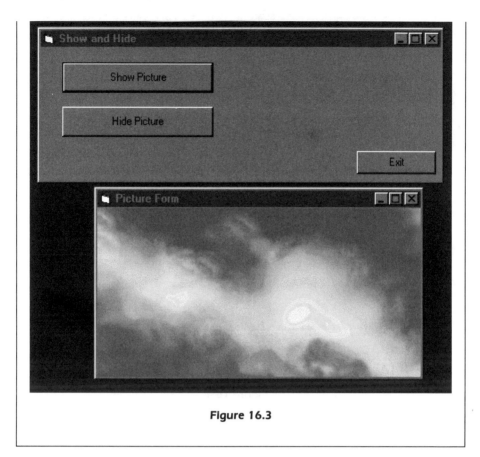

Figure 16.3

Start-up form

Normally, the first form added to the project will be the one which is automatically loaded when the project is run. If you have many forms in one application, it is possible to change the start-up form to any form within the project. This is useful if you later add an initial splash screen to your project, or a form with a menu system as in the task above.

To change the start-up form:

- Select **Project 1 Properties** from the **Project** menu, as in Figure 16.4.
- Use the Startup object drop-down list box to select the required form.
- Click on OK.

Now when you run the project, the selected form will be displayed.

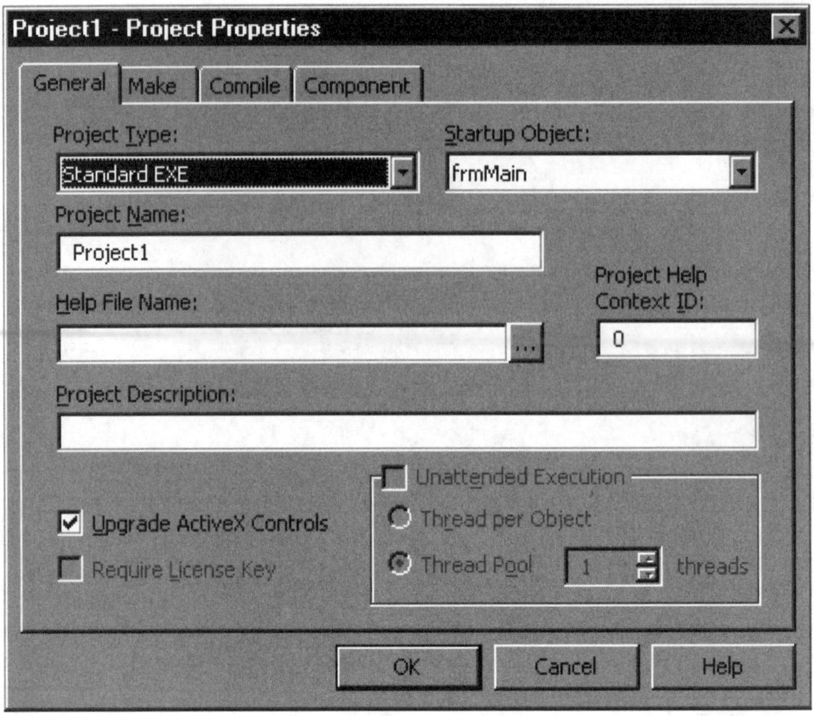

Figure 16.4

Older versions of Visual Basic accessed the Startup Form option from **Options** on the **Tools** menu. The option is located under the **Projects** tab.

Accessing properties

So far you have only seen properties referred to as object.property. In order for you to be able to access and change properties on a different form, the syntax used is:

form.object.property

For example, the background color of a label control on a different form would be referred to as:

frmName.lblMain.BackColor

> The form name can be omitted from the start of the syntax if you are referring to the current form.

If you hide a form its properties are still available. If, however, you Unload the form, its properties are no longer available. If a form which has been unloaded from memory is reloaded its properties are reset to their default values.

Availability of variables

If a variable is declared in the (General) (Declarations) section of a form, it is available throughout that form, but it is not available for use by other forms in the same project. If you want a variable to be available in more than one form, it must be declared at a higher level – in a module. This will be explained in more detail in Chapter 17.

Summary

In this chapter you have:

- added additional forms
- switched between forms
- learnt about use of variables across forms.

Subroutines, functions and modules

So far, your projects have consisted of code written for events which are associated with controls. Sometimes you will want to write code which can be used in more than one part of the application. This sort of code is written in a Visual Basic *subroutine* or *module*.

Subroutines

What is a subroutine?

All the Visual Basic code that you write is split up into individual subroutines, shortened to Sub. You have already encountered many of these – each event for a control is a separate subroutine.

Structure of subroutines

Subroutines belong to a form. They can either be event procedures for a control on the form, or they can be special user-created subroutines. When the program is run and a subroutine is activated the control of the program immediately switches to the line after the Private Sub line. After the End Sub line is encountered control is passed back to the calling line.

A subroutine provides a good way of accessing the same piece of code from more than one place. For example, if you have provided a command button and a menu option which do the same thing, the same code will be required in two places. To avoid duplicating the code in two places, you can create a subroutine to perform the action and make the command button and menu item both call the subroutine. This also makes changing the code easier because you only have to change it in one place, reducing the possibility of errors.

Adding a subroutine

Choose **Add Procedure . . .** from the **Tools** menu. You can only do this when the cursor is positioned in a code window. You will see a dialog box as in Figure 17.1.

In Visual Basic versions 3 and 4, select **Procedure . . .** from the **Insert** menu instead.

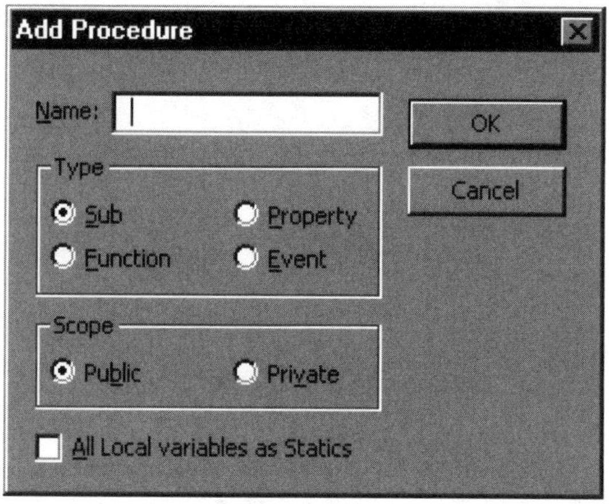

Figure 17.1

The name should be something memorable. The Scope of the procedure specifies from where in the program it is accessible:

- Public subs are available from any part of the project.
- Private subs are only accessible from within the same form.

Most subs are Private. It is better to put Public subs in a module because then they can be accessed even when the form is not loaded. See the Modules section below for further information.

You should leave the type as Sub for the moment: functions will be covered later.

Click on OK and you will see a blank subroutine, as shown in Figure 17.2. The procedure is placed in the (General) area. You can write the code in the subroutine in exactly the same way as normal.

Calling subroutines

There is no point in being able to create subroutines if it is then not possible to activate the code you have written. This is what the Call statement is used for. The syntax is:

Call procedurename

That's all there is to it – just Call and then the name of the procedure. For example, if you wanted to set up an Add command button and an Add menu item, both would contain the following:

Call Add

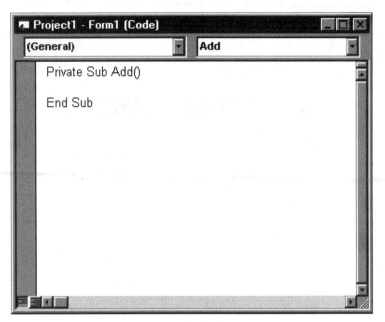

Figure 17.2

Passing parameters

Parameters are variables which can be passed to a procedure. Normally, the only variables available in a procedure are variables declared in the Declarations section of the form. However, you can pass any variable as a parameter and then access and use it in the subroutine.

To do this, there are two steps:

- In the procedure, the variables which you want to pass should be listed in brackets after the name, as in Figure 17.3.

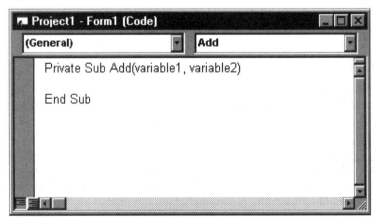

Figure 17.3

- When the subroutine is called, it should be called with the variables you want to pass in brackets after the name, as in Figure 17.4.

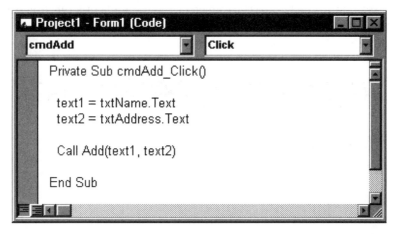

Figure 17.4

The variables text1 and text2 which normally would not have been available to the subroutine are now available for use. Inside the Add procedure text1 will be stored in variable1 and text2 in variable2.

> The variable names you pass to a subroutine do not have to be the same as the ones used in the subroutine.

> If a variable which is passed to a subroutine is changed by the subroutine, the variable retains its new value when control is passed back to the calling procedure.

Functions

You have already met functions in Chapter 9. These were all Visual Basic standard functions. You can, however, create your own functions.

A function is similar to a subroutine but is used in a different way. The principal difference is that a subroutine performs an action (maybe changing the screen display) whereas a function returns a value. For this reason, functions are used a lot in mathematical programs.

To create a function, use the same method as for a subroutine, except you should choose Function from the option buttons in the Add Procedure dialog shown in Figure 17.1. All functions have parameters passed to them (see the previous section for how to pass parameters). An example of a function is shown in Figure 17.5.

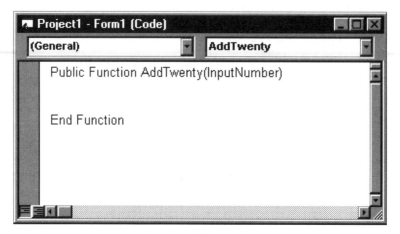

Figure 17.5

The result of executing the function (the return value) is returned by setting the name of the function to the value you want to return. For example, the function in Figure 17.6 will return the number passed to the program plus twenty.

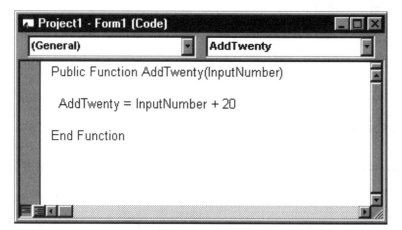

Figure 17.6

The function is used in the same way as you use standard Visual Basic functions. An example of how to use the function is shown in Figure 17.7. This simple example takes a number from a text box and, when the button is clicked, displays the input number plus twenty in the label.

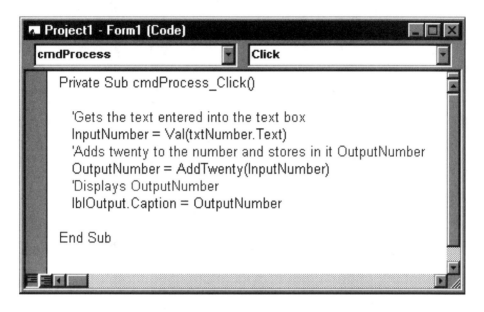

Figure 17.7

Task 17.1   Weight converter

This project will display a list of weights in pounds and their equivalent in kilograms.

In a new project, place a list box (long and thin) and a command button on to a form. Label the command button Go! An example is shown in Figure 17.8.

Create a function called PoundToKilogram. It will have one variable passed to it: the weight in pounds, and will return the kilogram equivalent.

The conversion formula is:
divide the number of pounds by 2.2 to get the number of kilograms.

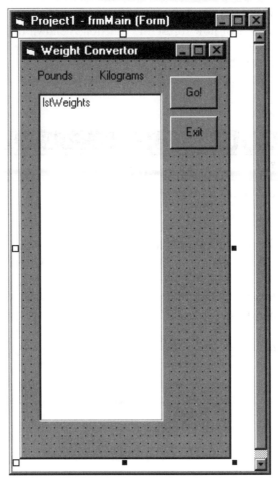

Figure 17.8

Add code to the Go! button so that when you click on it, a loop is activated which cycles through all weights in pounds between 0 and 200 in steps of 5 (check back to Chapter 11). For each weight, add a line to the list box quoting the weight in pounds and then the kilogram equivalent.

You can get two columns in a list box by using a Tab which can be inserted using Chr(9).

Add a format string to the Kilogram value so that values are rounded to one decimal place. An example is shown in Figure 17.9.

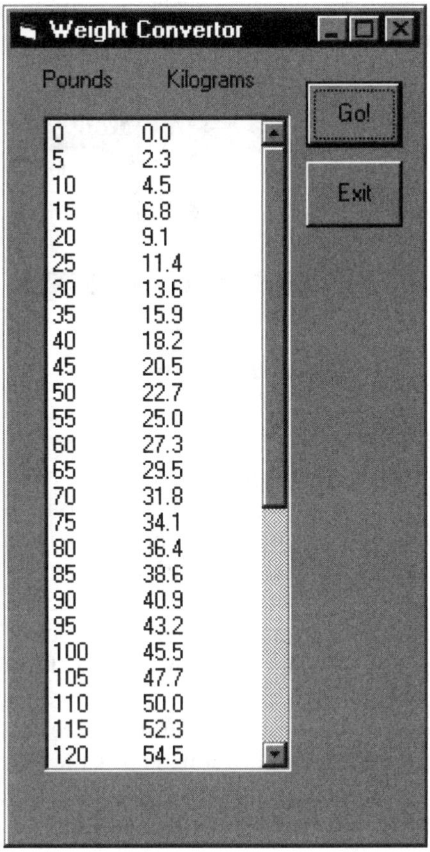

Figure 17.9

Modules

What is a module?

A module is a set of procedures and declarations which are stored in a single file separate from the rest of the code which is attached to forms and controls. The module does not contain any forms or controls. The module is stored as a separate file with a BAS extension. Modules are used where code is required by more than one form in the project.

Where does all this fit in?

You may be finding all these projects, forms, modules, subroutines and controls a bit confusing. The diagram in Figure 17.10 should help to simplify the way the components fit together to form the project.

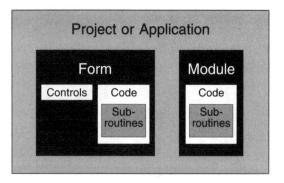

Figure 17.10

Use of modules

Modules are loaded when the application is run and stay open until the application is closed. Because of this, modules can contain code which is called from many different parts of your application. These calls can be anywhere throughout the various forms of the application.

Code is placed in a module when it needs to be accessed by more than one form. This could be a standard routine, such as a validation routine which is used by more than one form, or it could be a complicated function which is used by many parts of the program.

Variables declared as Public in the declarations section of a module are also available for use throughout the application. This is the most useful attribute of a module: variables can be used across forms. Usually variables declared in the form declarations section is available only to that form. If you want to transfer information across forms the variables must be declared in a module.

Adding a module

Click on the arrow to the right of the 🗈 ▾ button on the toolbar and then choose Module, or else select **Add Module** from the **Project** menu. Either way will display a window, as in Figure 17.11.

This allows you to select the type of module you want to insert, and includes any additional pre-setup modules. The ⚛ icon gives a standard code form, as in Figure 17.12.

> Users of Visual Basic versions 3 and 4 do not have a **Project** menu. Instead click on **Module** from the **Insert** menu. Also, you will not see a window as in Figure 17.11 – a code window as in Figure 17.12 will be displayed immediately instead.

The code window works in the same way as for Forms. You can code subroutines in the normal way (refer back to see the section on Subroutines earlier in the chapter).

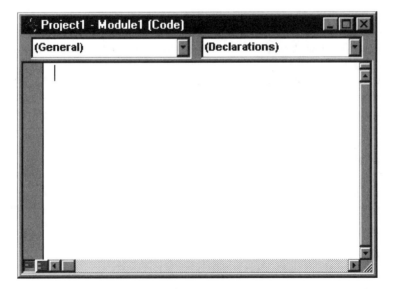

Figure 17.11

Figure 17.12

Declaring variables

There are three types of variables which you can use in a module:

- Temporary variables not declared in the declarations section and just used inside a procedure.
- Variables declared using a Private statement in the Declarations section of the module. These are available to all subroutines in the module.
- Variables declared as Public in the Declarations section of a module. These are available throughout the project and can be accessed and changed from anywhere. This is the most useful type of variable for a module.

The Public and Private statements are used in the same way as a Dim statement. The syntax is:

Public varname As Type

This would make the variable available throughout the project.

Private varname As Type

This would make the variable available only to subroutines in the module.

Task 17.2   Horse race

Create two forms. The first is a betting screen, as shown in Figure 17.13. This enables the user to select which horse they want to back. The odds sheet is set up randomly. The "Start Race" button closes down the betting form and displays the race form.

A module is required to store the number of the horse that has been backed and the odds. This information needs to be carried through to the next form, so the variables must be declared as Public in a module.

The next screen has four horses which move across the screen. The best way of creating this is to put the movement on a timer, and make it randomly choose which horse should move.

The winner is the one which reaches the right-hand edge first. An example is shown in Figure 17.14.

After the race is complete, a message box should be displayed showing how much the user has won or lost. The game should then re-start.

Possible improvements:

- Make the longer odds horses less likely to win
- Keep a running total of money
- Let the user choose how much to bet.

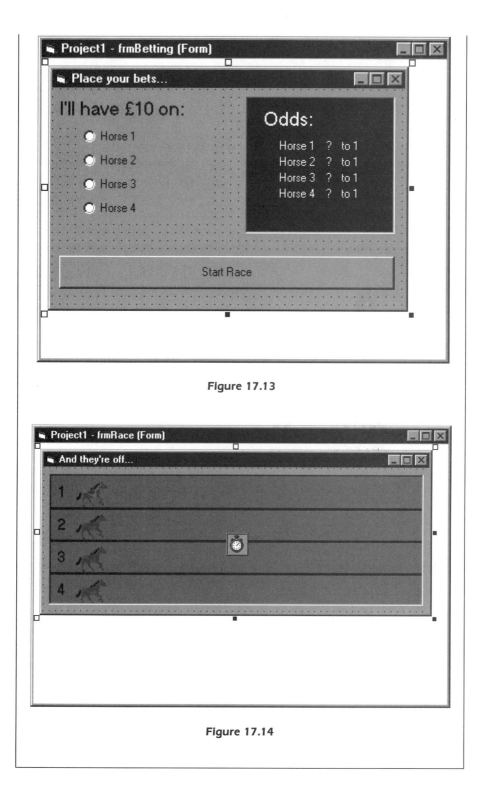

Figure 17.13

Figure 17.14

Summary

In this chapter you have:

- added subroutines to forms
- used functions
- added modules to a project
- learnt about availability of variables between different parts of the project.

Putting it all together

At this stage in the book you have gained many skills in using Visual Basic. You have created a good number of small applications whilst working through the material in the book. Real applications are usually quite a lot more complex than these examples. This chapter builds a real application so you can see how all the skills you have learnt can be used and combined. The application is developed in stages with an explanation of what is happening at each stage. Hints are suggested for solving the various problems you will come across. Bear in mind that even experienced programmers find that applications can present problems that prove difficult to solve.

The full code is also provided so you can check your programming as you work through the project. Most projects can be coded in many different ways. This project is no exception and you may have done things differently from the suggested solution. You can compare your way with the suggested method – and may well find that yours is better! This is the essence of the skill of programming.

Planning a project

Every project has to be planned. The stages that you will go through are:

- Analyze the tasks involved and the sequence in which they happen.
- Design the forms.
- Set the properties.
- Write the code.
- Test the program and make improvements.

Before starting to write code it is a good idea to check the form design with the people who will use the program. Projects created for publication or for other people whether for commercial or leisure reasons will need a user guide to back up the use of the program. You will want to supply the program in a form where it can be used without Visual Basic. This is easy to do using the Visual Basic application wizard. You can find details of this in the appendices.

The Hangman project

This project takes you through creating a Hangman game using Visual Basic. In this format, Hangman is a game for two players: one player chooses a word and then the other has to guess the word.

Analyze the tasks

The program will have to:

- allow a word or words to be entered
- display the word as a series of asterisks (*) or hyphens (-)
- allow letters to be guessed correctly
- check the letter against the correct word
- replace the characters with correct letters
- build up gallows and man for incorrect letters
- detect when a word has been guessed correctly
- detect when the man has been hung
- allow players to end the game
- reset the screen for another game

Designing the forms and controls

The project has two main parts: entering the word and guessing the word. The word can be entered using an input box. Using this method means that controls are not needed on the form. Another way of entering the word is to use a text box which is made visible at the start of the project then hidden after the word has been entered. If you do it this way the text box will need to be drawn on the form. The guessing part of the project can be done on a single form. You may want to add extra forms nearer the end of the project.

Guessing the letters   You have to find a way of allowing player 2 to guess letters. This can be done in a number of ways. One way would be to use a text box into which the letter is typed. Another method is to display the letters on command buttons which then just have to be clicked to input the letter. This is easier and more fun for the user. It also has to avoid having to check for both lower and upper case letters. The screen will need 26 command buttons with captions A to Z. These are grouped in a control array cmdLetter where the command button with index 0 is A, index is B and so on to index 25 which is Z.

Displaying the word   There needs to be somewhere to display the asterisks at the start of the game which then shows the word as it is guessed. The best way of doing this is to use a label control which will initially contain a set of blanks, but which will be filled in as the user guesses the letters. The label control is named lblGuess and its color and font properties are set to add interest.

Drawing the man   The main form also has to have an area where the gallows and the man are drawn. There are different approaches to drawing the man, but the simplest is to create a set of gallows and a man out of shape controls. The controls are all of the same type so a control array can be used for this. The indices of the shapes should be in the order that they will be displayed, so index 0 is the bottom of the gallows through to the last shape used for the man. When the game starts, the gallows and man should not be displayed so the Visible properties of the shapes are all set to False.

An example of the form is shown in Figure 18.1. In this example, the gallows and man are made up of nine shapes which is about right for the number of guesses that are allowed. You could start with part of the gallows displayed on the form and then build the rest of the gallows and the man.

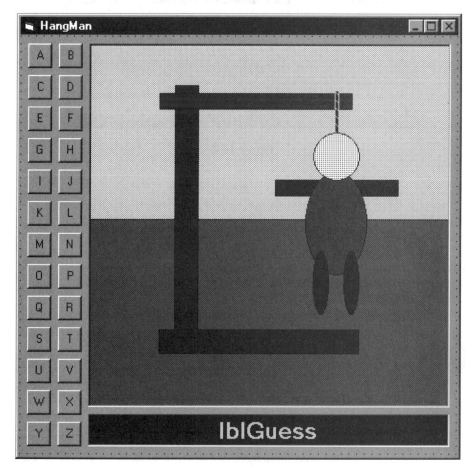

Figure 18.1

Writing the code

Starting the project The project needs to load the main form and allow the game to be started. The first thing to be done is to allow player 1 to input the word to be guessed. This can be done quite easily using an input box.

Inputting the word to be guessed The word to be guessed is entered by Player 1. In an input box ask the other player to look away, while Player 1 enters a word. This should be coded in the Form Load procedure so that it appears when the program is started. An example is shown in Figure 18.2.

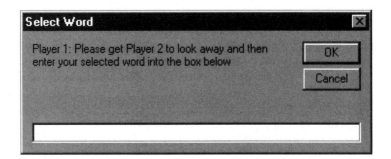

Figure 18.2

Processing the input The variable into which the word is entered needs to be available throughout the form so it should be declared in the (declarations) section of the form.

You don't know how player 1 will type the word; it could be a mixture of small and capital letters. To make it easier to check, all the letters should be converted to upper-case using the UCase function. You can convert the word to upper-case and store it in the same variable.

Once the word has been entered, the program needs to find out how many letters are in the word and display that number of asterisks or other characters in the label control lblGuess. The String function allows the same character to be put into a string a set number of times.

The syntax is:

String (numberoftimes, character)

The numberoftimes should be the length of the word entered by player 1. The character is the * or -.

For a six-letter word, the label control lblGuess would look like Figure 18.3.

Figure 18.3

Try coding this and then run and test your program. If you get really stuck, you can find one way of doing this in the suggested solution. When you have made the program work so far, carry on with the next tasks.

The next part to code is the command buttons on the form which are used for selecting a letter. When one of these is clicked, you need to check whether the letter is contained in the word which has been entered. This word is now stored in upper-case letters in a variable within the program. If the letter is contained in the word, it should be shown in lblGuess in the correct place. There may be more than one occurrence of the letter in the word. If so, all the occurrences need to be replaced. If the letter is not contained in the word, the next part of the man and gallows should be drawn. After a letter has been selected, the button should be disabled so the user cannot choose the same letter again.

Finding out which letter has been guessed When the user clicks on one of the letter buttons, the Index property gives the number of the control in the control array. This will be from 0 for A to 25 for Z. The Index value needs to be converted to its corresponding letter. The Chr function can be used to do this:

Letter = Chr(Index + 65)

Checking the letter guessed The best way to check if the letter is contained within the word is to use a For Next loop to check the letter against each of the letters in the word. The Mid function will extract an individual letter from the word.

If the letter is found in the word, it needs to be replaced in the label control lblGuess. To do this, you will need to find out the position of the letter in the string. You know this from the Mid function. You will then need to replace the character at that position in lblGuess making sure that you keep all the letters which have already been replaced.

An example might help! If the word is BANANA and so far the B has been guessed lblGuess would be B*****.

If the letter N is guessed, this is what needs to happen. The computer finds the first N when at position 3. It then takes the left two characters from the guess box (B*), adds the letter N, and then takes the right-hand portion of the string (***). This leaves the guess box as B*N***. The computer continues searching through the string, and does the same thing for the other N to give B*N*N*.

Have a go at coding this part of the program. This is one of the trickiest parts so don't worry if it takes you several attempts! Keep running the program and testing your code. Again, if you need help, the solution is at the end of the chapter.

Drawing the gallows and man If the loop has completed without the guessed letter being found, you need to draw the next part of the man and gallows. To work out which is the next bit of the gallows to be drawn, a NextPart variable is required. This should be set to zero in the Form Load procedure, and has to be declared in (Declarations) so it is available throughout the form. Now, when the letter is not found, the NextPart variable is used to make the next part of the man and gallows visible. You then need to add one to NextPart.

Run and test this part of the program. An example of a part-drawn gallows is shown in Figure 18.4.

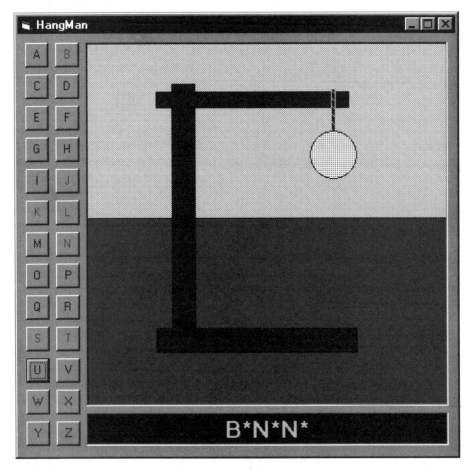

Figure 18.4

Winning and losing The project is now nearly complete! All that is required is a win and lose part. You win if you guess all the letters in the word before the gallows are complete. You lose when the gallows are complete and the word has not been correctly guessed.

The best way to test for a win is to check whether lblGuess is the same as the word that was entered and is stored in the variable. If they are the same, player 2 has won. The game is lost if the man is complete. You can check for this by looking at the NextPart variable. If this has reached 9, player 2 has lost. Note that the value will change according to the number of components in your man/gallows control array.

Add the code to program the win and lose. At its simplest level, you could have a message box saying You Win or You Lose.

The basic Hangman game is now complete and hopefully working. Challenge your friends to several games and then impress them all by telling them you wrote it!

Further enhancements:

- Add playing instructions.
- Add an option for another game on the Win and Lose boxes. These will have to reset the gallows and the letter buttons, as well as ask for another word.
- Add a menu to the program – options could be New game, Exit and Help which brings up the instructions.
- Add a clock to the screen showing how long it has taken.
- Add a Give Up button!
- Improve the graphics with more color.
- Make it work if more than one word is entered.
- Add Win and Lose forms. These will be more impressive than merely saying Win or Lose. An example is shown in Figure 18.5.

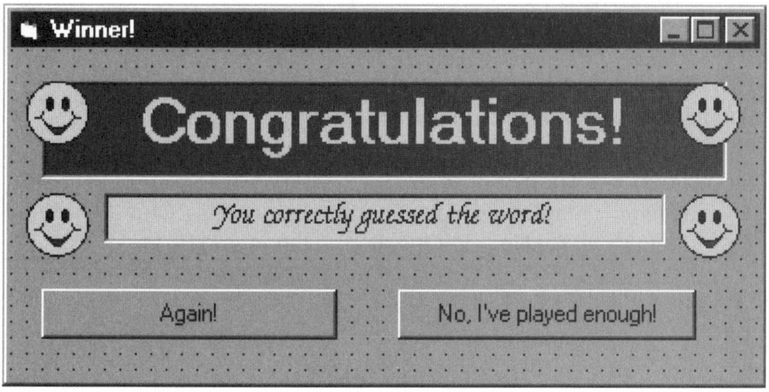

Figure 18.5

A solution

```
Dim word As String
Dim nextpart As Integer
```

```
Private Sub cmdLetter_Click(Index As Integer)
    cmdLetter(Index).Enabled = False

    'Change index to appropriate letter
    letter = Chr(Index + 65)

    'Check for letter in word
    If InStr(word, letter) <> 0 Then
        'If in word
        GuessString = lblGuess.Caption
        For currentplace = 1 To Len(word)
            If letter = Mid(word, currentplace, 1) Then
                GuessString = Left(GuessString, currentplace - 1) + letter +
                Mid(GuessString, currentplace + 1)
            End If
        Next
        lblGuess.Caption = GuessString
        'Check if lblGuess if the same as the entered word
        If lblGuess.Caption = word Then
            answer = MsgBox("Well done! You saved the man." + Chr(13) + "Play
            again?", vbYesNo + vbQuestion, "Hangman")
            If answer = 6 Then Call NewGame Else End
        End If
    Else
        'Draw gallows/man
        shpGalMan(nextpart).Visible = True
        nextpart = nextpart + 1
        If nextpart = 9 Then
            answer = MsgBox("Oops. The man is dead." + Chr(13) + "Play
            again?", vbYesNo + vbQuestion, "Hangman")
            If answer = 6 Then Call NewGame Else End
        End If
    End If
End Sub
```

```
Private Sub NewGame()
    nextpart = 0
    word = InputBox("Player 1: Please get Player 2 to look away and then enter
    your selected word into the box below", "Select Word")
    "Switch on all letters
    For i = 0 To 25
        cmdLetter(i).Enabled = True
    Next
    "Display no gallows/man
    For i = 0 To 8
        shpGalMan(i).Visible = False
    Next
    word = Trim(UCase(word))
    lblGuess.Caption = String(Len(word), "*")
End Sub
Private Sub Form_Load()
```

```
Call NewGame
End Sub
```

Practising your skills

Stop watch

Your computer has a clock inside it. This can be used as an accurate stop watch.

The Stop Watch will start timing when the user clicks Go! When the Stop! button is clicked, the program will show the Stop time and the elapsed time.

Start a new project, and create a form as shown in Figure 19.1.

```
┌─ Stop Watch ──────────────────── _ □ ✕ ─┐
│                                           │
│  ┌─────────┐    Start time    ┌─────────┐ │
│  │   Go!   │                  │         │ │
│  └─────────┘    End time      ┌─────────┐ │
│  ┌─────────┐                  │         │ │
│  │  Stop!  │                  ──────────  │
│  └─────────┘                              │
│                 Elapsed time  ┌─────────┐ │
│                               │         │ │
└───────────────────────────────────────────┘
```

Figure 19.1

The three boxes at the right of the form are labels which have had their captions deleted.

There are two ways to create this timer program:

The Time function could be used to give the current time in the Start time and End time boxes and then a subtraction performed to find the elapsed time.

The Timer function could be used. This gives the number of seconds elapsed since midnight correct to the nearest hundredth of a second. This method creates a more accurate stop watch.

Add code to the Go! button so that it places the current timer value in the start label.

Add code to the Stop! button so that when you click on it, it displays the timer value in the end box, and calculates the elapsed time. This is displayed in the third label.

Run and test the program. An example is shown in Figure 19.2.

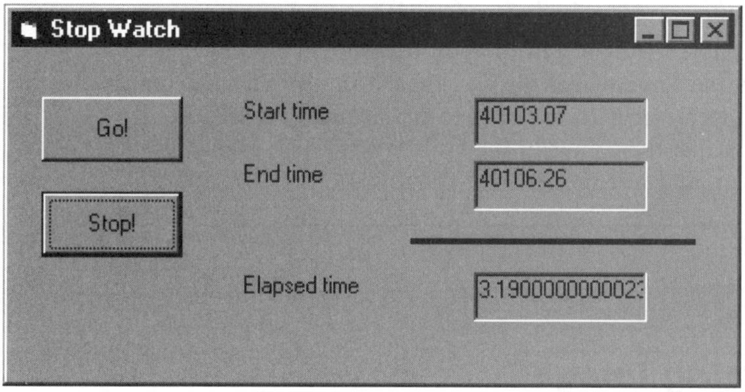

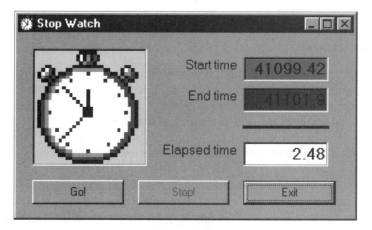

Figure 19.2

You will notice that the Elapsed time box shows many decimal places. The value needs to be rounded to the nearest hundredth of a second. The Format statement can be used to do this.

The form at the moment looks a little dull: you can liven it up using images and colors like that shown in Figure 19.3.

Add code to the Go! button so that all the times are blanked out before the start of a new timing.

Set Enabled for the Stop! button to False at design time.

In the Go! button code enable the Stop! button and disable the Go! button.

In the Stop! button code enable the Go! button and disable the Stop! button.

Figure 19.3

Run and test the program again. OK so far?

Currently, the elapsed time is only displayed when the Stop! button is clicked. An improvement would be to continually update the elapsed time as the stop watch was running. To do this, you need to add a Timer control to the form. Set the Timer interval to 10 (this calls the Timer event every hundredth of a second). Set the enabled property of the Timer to False.

Enable the Timer in the Go! button Click event.

In the Timer event, display the current Timer value minus the start time value. Remember to round it to the nearest hundredth.

Disable the Timer in the Go! button Click event.

Run and test the finished program.

Spinning Image

Be the envy of all your friends with a personalized screen saver! This project shows you how to create a working screen saver which you can adopt as your standard Windows screen saver.

The screen saver will feature a spinning picture in the centre of the screen, and this picture can be anything of your choice, from your name to your favourite picture!

Start a new project. The following properties of the form need setting:

- BorderStyle to None so the form can take up all the screen.
- BackColor to a color of your choice – black works well for screen savers.
- WindowStyle to Maximized so that the form takes up all the screen when loaded.
- Caption to blank to remove the title bar.
- ControlBox to False.
- MaxButton and MinButton to False (only needed in earlier versions of Visual Basic).

You can try running this project. It should give a completely blank screen, with no title bar and no task bar. Use Ctrl-Break followed by End from the Run menu to stop the program.

Add an image control to the centre of the form.

Now you have to decide what picture you want on the form. This can be any existing graphic file or you can create your own pictures using a drawing or painting program such as the Windows Paint program.

You can either copy a picture to the clipboard and paste it into the image control, or else save it and then load the picture into the Picture property of the image control. Either way will give you a picture in an image control, as in Figure 19.4.

Figure 19.4

The image is made to spin by setting the Stretch property to True and then changing the width of the image. This produces the spinning effect. This has the added advantage that is also possible to make your initial starting image as large as you like. The width of the image is changed through a series of steps controlled by a Timer control. Call it tmrSpin. Enable the timer and set its Interval to 1 (the smallest possible).

In the Form Load procedure, store the original width of the image in a variable and set a direction variable to -1. This variable will indicate whether the image is increasing or decreasing in size. Initially the image starts at full size and decreases so the variable is negative. The variables (original width and direction) must be declared in the (General) (Declarations) section so they are available throughout the form.

To the Timer event, add code to:

- Set the new width 100 more than the previous if the direction is positive, otherwise set it to 100 less.
- Add an If command to check that the new width is not less than zero. If it is, set the width to 1 and change the direction.
- Add an If command to check that the new width is not greater than the original width (stored in a variable in Form Load). If it is, reverse the direction.
- Change the width of the image to the calculated width value.

Run and test it in its current form. The picture should appear to grow and shrink from the left of the image which remains still.

The project is now almost complete except that the image needs to be seen to rotate rather than shrink and grow. The way to do this is to make the stationary point the centre line of the image instead of the left-hand side. The width variable stays the same but you will also need a new variable to give the position of the left-hand edge of the image.

The left variable differs from the width because if the width is decreasing the left property should be increasing. Also, the left property should have half the amount added to it that the width does (otherwise it would rotate around a fixed right-hand edge). Therefore you should add 50 to the new left variable, and multiply it by -1 and the direction. Complicated! An example is:

```
NewLeft = imgSpin.Left + 50 * direction * -1
```

Run and test the program. You should now have a working spinning image rotating around its centre.

The final stage of the project is to make the screen disappear at the right time. Add code so that whenever a key is pressed, or the mouse is clicked, the program ends. This needs the End command in the relevant event procedures for the form.

Run and test the program to see if it ends at the correct time.

Possible improvements:

- Make the image reverse (you will need another image which is the reverse of the first image to switch on).
- Move the image around the screen as well as spinning.
- Add a password.

It is possible to turn this into a working Windows screensaver. The Microsoft web site and KeyFax services have instructions about how to do this.

Name reversal

Have you ever wondered what your name would look like backwards? No? Well here's your chance!

This project will take the letters of a word or phrase and reverse them, so "Hello World" would become "dlroW olleH".

Start a new project and create a form which contains a text box. Add a command button marked Reverse, as in Figure 19.5.

Figure 19.5

Write code to swap the order of the letters in the Reverse button. The stages you will need to code are:

- Count the number of letters.
- Loop through all the letters starting with the last and finishing with the first (a STEP -1 on the end of a For command will do this or you can use a Do .. Loop to count backwards).
- Take each letter and add it to the start of a new string (the Mid function takes individual letters from a string).
- Display the new string in the place of the old one in the text box.

Run and test the program. You may need to go back and work through your reversal logic several times before it works properly. If you click on the button twice, you should see what you started with, as in Figure 19.6.

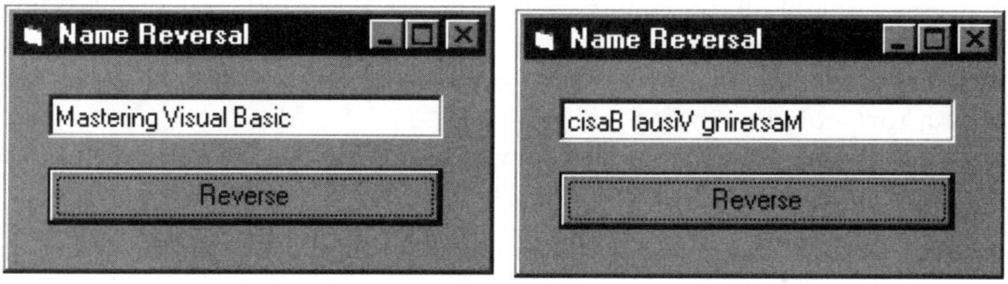

Figure 19.6

Add a check so that an error message is displayed and text has to be re-entered if there are less than two characters in the text box.

Add an Exit button to the form and smarten it up by using colors and fonts, as in Figure 19.7.

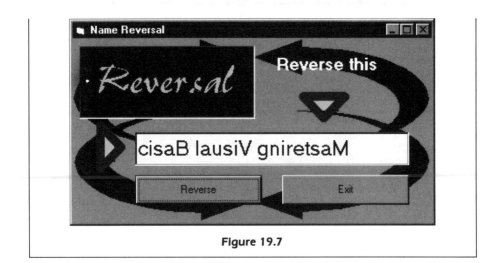

Figure 19.7

Noughts and Crosses

The last project is a version of Noughts and Crosses. Graphically easy to do, but the logic to make the computer play well is complicated.

You will require a control array of nine images. These will form the playing board. Also, a three-by-three array of integer values is required. This will be used for all the calculations.

A sample form design is shown in Figure 19.8. The X and O at the right are invisible images which are used as a store for the O and X symbols.

When the user clicks in a square, a O needs putting in the square. The computer then must decide where it should play. A way of deciding is shown below:

- Choose a random free square. This is the default square to play unless it is overridden by one of the below.
- Stop the user winning by looking for rows with two Os and a blank square in a row, column or diagonal.
- Check to see if the computer can win – look for two Xs and a blank square.

These are listed in reverse order of importance. If the computer can win, it should. Otherwise it should stop the user winning, otherwise it chooses a random square. This logic does not produce an infallible game of noughts and crosses, but it wins or draws most games. A computer that won every time would just depress the player anyway!

This logic is quite tricky to code. You will need to use subroutines to do the checking for you.

The next step is to see whether the user or the computer has won, or if the game is drawn when the board is filled and neither side has won.

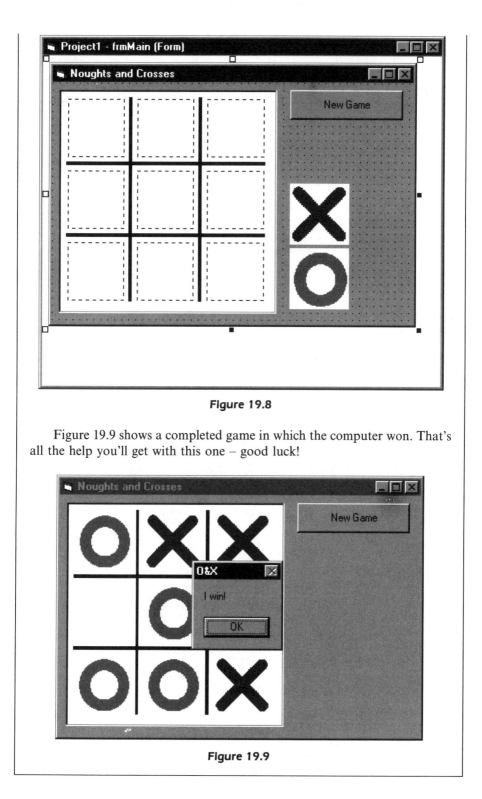

Figure 19.8

Figure 19.9 shows a completed game in which the computer won. That's all the help you'll get with this one – good luck!

Figure 19.9

Appendix A: Books Online

Earlier versions of Visual Basic came with large numbers of printed manuals which nobody ever read! Visual Basic version 5 comes with all the documentation supplied on the CD. The Books Online application is used to read and search the documentation.

Starting Books Online

Select the **Search Master Index . . .** option from the **Help** menu in Visual Basic. Books Online is also referenced from some help pages. The first screen of Books Online is shown in Figure A.1.

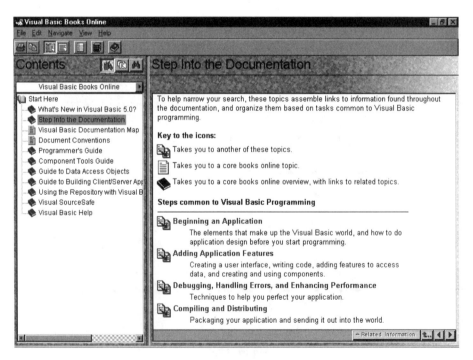

Figure A.1

Using Books Online

The left-hand window gives you a list of books included with the package. If you double-click a book, it opens and the contents can be read. Subsequent double-clicking opens chapters which you can view in the right-hand window. An example is shown in Figure A.2.

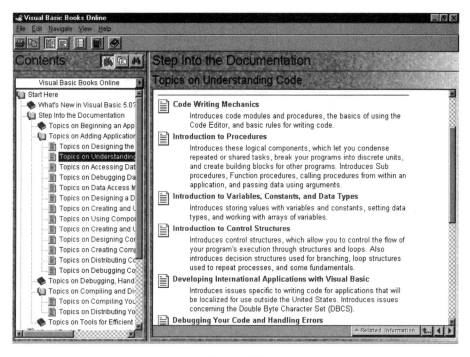

Figure A.2

Any writing in green in the right-hand window is a hotlink, similar to those used in the Help system. Clicking on these will take you to another document.

Searching Books Online

The Index button ▣ allows you to search the Visual Basic help system. Far more useful is the Find button ▥ which searches through all the books for topics relating to the text you enter. An example Find is shown in Figure A.3. From here you can jump directly to any of the documents relating to your search.

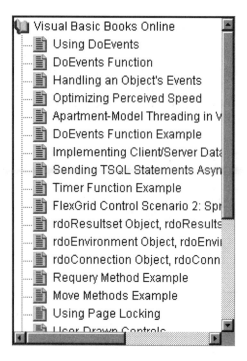

Figure A.3

Appendix B: Creating EXE files from projects

The Microsoft software licence prohibits copying of Visual Basic, so if you want to distribute any of your applications you have to create an EXE file. An EXE file is an executable file created from your project which will run without Visual Basic on the computer.

Creating an EXE file

Select the **Make ProjectName.EXE . . .** option from the **File** menu. This will display a dialog box as shown in Figure B.1.

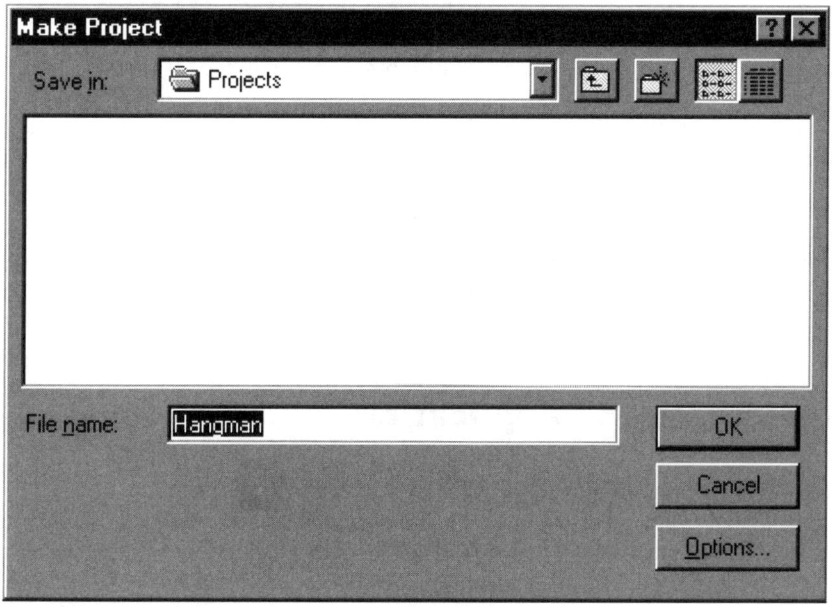

Figure B.1

This lets you choose the name of the EXE file for your project, and also its location. The Options. . . buttons lets you change many different aspects of the EXE file. The Project Properties dialog is shown in Figure B.2.

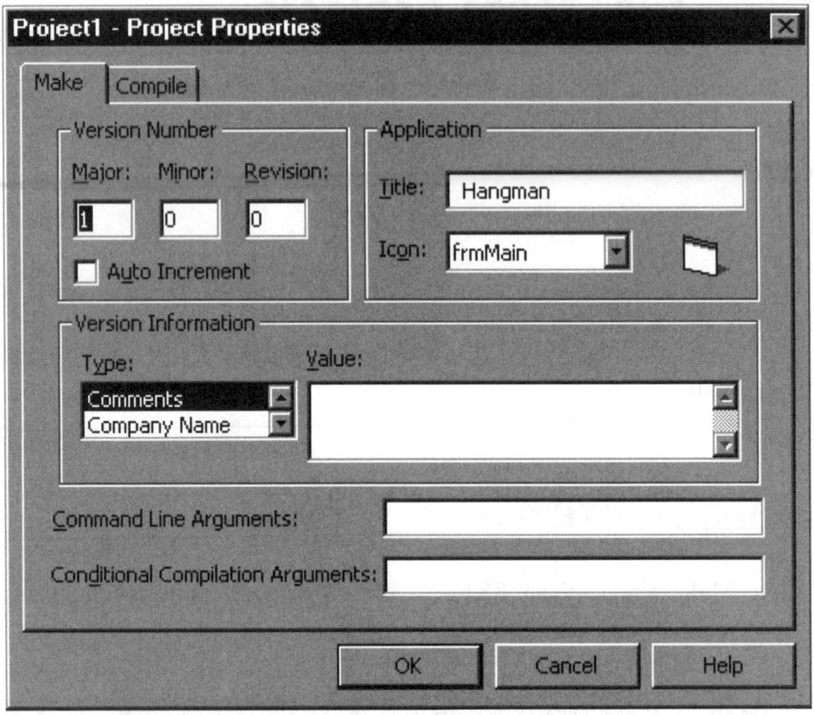

Figure B.2

You can set the version number, the application title and its icon. The Compile tab gives you access to more advanced options connected with the way the program is compiled into an EXE file.

Click OK from the Make Project dialog and after a short time the project will be compiled into an EXE file. You can try running this EXE and you will find that it can be run without loading Visual Basic.

Distributing the application

Although it is compiled into an EXE file, this EXE file will not work on its own. You need to supply DLL (dynamic link library) files with it. DLL files contain instructions used by Visual Basic. The number of DLLs you have to distribute with your application varies according to the complexity of the application. You also need to supply any OCX (custom control files) which you have used in your application.

It is very tricky trying to find all these files. The Setup Wizard supplied with Visual Basic leads you through this process and automatically locates all the files you have used. The Setup Wizard (if installed) appears in the Visual Basic group on the Start menu (or in Program Manager). The first screen of the Application Setup Wizard is shown in Figure B.3.

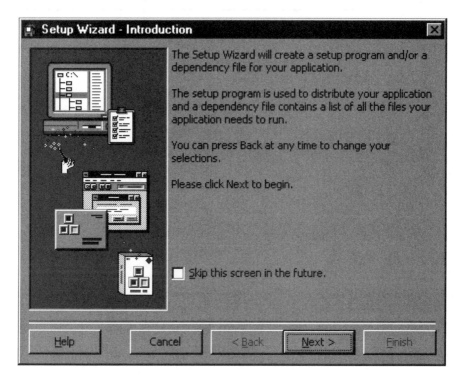

Figure B.3

The Setup Wizard also produces distribution disks at the end and writes a very good Setup program for the application. It leads you through all the steps required to distribute your application to other people.

Microsoft lets you distribute the DLLs free of charge. If you have used any other add-ons, check that they can also be distributed.

Appendix C: Visual Basic world wide web sites

The Visual Basic Help menu has links to Microsoft's world wide web sites. The list below has some further Visual Basic sites available on the world wide web. The links pages are good places to start as they link to far more places than we can in this book.

Microsoft's main Visual Basic site

http://www.microsoft.com/vbasic/

A superb resource for news, software and add-ons to Visual Basic.

Microsoft's Visual Basic support wizard

http://www.microsoft.com/VBasicSupport/

This gives access to the Visual Basic Knowledge Base. This is a quick and cheap way of getting technical support, and has answers to thousands of questions.

Carl and Gary's Visual Basic page

http://www.apexsc.com/vb/

A very good in-depth site.

The Mother of All Visual Basic Web Sites Links

http://www.apexsc.com/vb/sites.html

The title says it all! This is a huge and well laid out set of Visual Basic links.

Inside Visual Basic for Windows

http://www.cobb.com/ivb/index.htm

The home page of the magazine.

Strollo Software's Most Comprehensive Visual Basic List

http://www.op.net/~jstrollo/vblinks.html

Another page of Visual Basic links.

Visual Basic on the Web

http://nautilus.utmb.edu/Visual Basic.htm

A very large site of Visual Basic links.

Ask the Visual Basic Pro

http://www.inquiry.com/thevbpro/index.html

A technical support page which has answers to many common questions. The Visual Basic Pro is also available to answer other queries by e-mail.

Index